WHO WAS ELEANOR RIGBY?...

and 908 More Questions and Answers about the Beatles

BRANDON TOROPOV

HarperPerennial
A Division of HarperCollinsPublishers

WHO WAS ELEANOR RIGBY?. . . AND 908 MORE QUESTIONS AND ANSWERS ABOUT THE BEATLES. Copyright © 1996 by Brandon Toropov. All rights reserved. Printed in the United States of America. No part of this book may be used or reproduced in any manner whatsoever without written permission except in the case of brief quotations embodied in critical articles and reviews. For information address HarperCollins Publishers, Inc., 10 East 53rd Street, New York, New York 10022.

HarperCollins books may be purchased for educational, business, or sales promotional use. For information, please write to: Special Markets Department, HarperCollins Publishers, Inc., 10 East 53rd Street, New York, New York 10022.

FIRST EDITION

Designed by Ruth Lee

Library of Congress Cataloging-in-Publication Data

Toropov, Brandon.
    Who was Eleanor Rigby?. . . and 908 more questions and answers about the Beatles / Brandon Toropov. — 1st ed.
Toropov, Brandon.
        p.   cm.
    ISBN 0-06-273442-3
    1. Beatles—Miscellanea.   I. Title.
ML421.B4T67   1997
782.42166'092'2—dc20   96-24982

96 97 98 99 00 ❖/RRD 10 9 8 7 6 5 4 3 2 1

To Julia Gail Toropov,
she who boasts seashell eyes and
shimmering hair of floating sky.

CONTENTS

ACKNOWLEDGMENTS

David Toropov and Meghan Tragert served as my assistants on this book. It was made more joyful and, not infrequently, more precise by the contributions and critiques of: Mary Toropov, Leslie Hamilton, Bob Tragert, Grace Hughes-Manor, and Mark Waldstein. It would have been impossible without Glenn KnicKrehm, to whom I am again in debt.

ILMP.

INTRODUCTION

Item the first, regarding what is to be found herein: This book offers 909 questions and answers—some easy, some not so easy—about the Beatles. (The number of questions has been selected for reasons of karmic symmetry that will become clear as you near the end of the book.) Most of the questions appear in sections keyed to a particular year of the band's career, but I've made no attempt to impose a strict chronological order within those sections. (In some cases, doing so would give away the answer to a question!) When deciding what year was most appropriate to connect to a recording, I've favored release dates over composition or recording dates. This means that questions about a song like "Two Of Us," which was part of the 1969 sessions for the album that would become *Let It Be*, would be included under the year 1970, when that LP was released.

Item the second, regarding the advisability of cheating: During group sessions, it's perfectly okay to sneak off to another room, buzz the answers, then return to your friends, read the questions out loud, and pretend you knew the answers all along and are hearing the questions for the first time.

Item the third, and lastly, regarding the best music in the world: The book is more fun if you're actually *listening* to Beatles CDs as you read it. (For what it's worth, I was listening to Beatles CDs as I wrote it.) Maybe the song you're trying to remember will start playing as you're reading the book. You never know.

Part of the fun of developing a real familiarity with the group's output and creative process lies in arguing about stuff with other Beatles people. If you want to argue about anything I've written here, please drop me a line, care of the publisher.

BRANDON TOROPOV

And now. . . here they are. . .

one
The Albums

Can you answer these questions about the Beatles' album releases—without appealing to your CD collection for help? (Answers begin on page 4.)

1 What was the first British-issue Beatles LP?

   A. *Please Please Me*
   B. *With The Beatles*
   C. *Beatles For Sale*

2 In November of 1963, the Beatles issued their second British album. It featured the "half-shadow" portrait that would also be used on the American release *Meet The Beatles!* Name the UK release.

3 In June of 1964, Polydor reissued the group's early Hamburg recordings backing up a British vocalist. The (padded) LP was called *The Beatles' First* in Britain. Name the singer who suddenly found himself receiving second billing to his former pickup band.

   A. Cliff Richard
   B. Tony Sheridan
   C. Lonnie Donegan

4 In July of 1964, the Beatles issued their third full-length British LP, the first Beatles album that featured no versions of songs by other artists. What was it called?

5 Late 1964 now. Looking a bit bedraggled on the cover sleeve, the Beatles dutifully slung together a collection of rather depressing originals, as well as some upbeat covers of American rock tunes, for their fourth British LP. It arrived in stores, coincidentally enough, just in time for Christmas. Name this album, which, though certainly appealing, is generally regarded as the least inspired of the Beatles' full-length British records.

6 The Beatles' next British album, released in August of 1965, featured the shortest title of any of the group's LPs. What was it called?

7 In contrast to its 1964 predecessor, the 1965 Beatles release for the Christmas selling season is acknowledged as one of the band's finest achievements. Despite the time pressure of these sessions—the band spent a single, profoundly harried month, from October 12 to November 11, 1965, at work on the project—the new release marked the Beatles' emergence as mature artists, rather than purveyors of catchy singles. What is the title of this magnificent "rush job"?

8 The Beatles' August 1966 LP marked George Harrison's emergence as a songwriter to be reckoned with; the album opened with one of his compositions. Name the LP.

9 The British version of the next Beatles LP featured, after the album's listed tracks, a high-pitched tone inaudible to humans (but clear as day to any dogs in the audience), and an "inner groove" of repeated chatter. What was the album called?

10 Early in the Beatles' career, American record companies developed remarkably skimpy soundtrack albums, released to take advantage of film projects, that featured a few tracks of Beatles music supplemented by orchestral/instrumental tunes of minimal interest to the group's fans. (The corresponding British releases contained roughly twice as much new Beatles music.) For the most part, the Beatles' British LP catalog evidences a disdain for this "accountant's maneuver"—but there is a soundtrack album released with the group's blessing in the UK and the States that is an even poorer value than the previous American soundtrack releases. Name it.

11 What Beatles LP features a wealth of songs composed while members of the band were on retreat in India?

12 The next all-new Beatles LP, which hit the stores in September of 1969, was the last one recorded—but *not* the group's final album release. Can you identify it?

13 The final album of all-new material released by the foursome was the long-delayed product of the *Get Back* sessions, and the only one of the group's recording efforts between 1963 and

1970 to be produced in its final version by someone other than George Martin. Name the album, and the man who took on the job of salvaging the *Get Back* tapes.

14 On the sleeve of one of the LPs mentioned above, the Beatles broke record-industry tradition by including the lyrics to their songs. Name the album.

15 Only one of the Beatles' LPs officially released between 1963 and 1970 consists entirely of Lennon/McCartney compositions. What was it?

    A. *A Hard Day's Night*
    B. *Sgt. Pepper's Lonely Hearts Club Band*
    C. *Let It Be*

Answers

1 a) *Please Please Me*

2 *With The Beatles*

3 b) Tony Sheridan

4 *A Hard Day's Night*

5 *Beatles For Sale*

6 *Help!*

7 *Rubber Soul*

8 *Revolver*

9 *Sgt. Pepper's Lonely Hearts Club Band*

10 The soundtrack album for the film *Yellow Submarine*, which features all of four new songs, the rest of the disc being occupied by previously released tracks and instrumentals recorded by other musicians.

11 *The Beatles* (a.k.a. *The White Album*)

12 *Abbey Road*

13 *Let It Be.* The album's final overseer—triage surgeon?—was Phil Spector.

14 *Sgt. Pepper's Lonely Hearts Club Band*

15 a) *A Hard Day's Night*

two

Sound Effects, Anyone?

T he Beatles' innovative use of sounds from the studio sound-effects library—and elsewhere—led to some memorable recorded moments. How many of the following can you identify? (Answers begin on page 8.)

16 A song on *Abbey Road* features the sound of a hammer clanging against a piece of metal. Which one is it?

    A. "Maxwell's Silver Hammer"
    B. "Something"
    C. "Her Majesty"

17 Name the Beatles song that features an alarm clock going off.

    A. "A Day In The Life"
    B. "Come Together"
    C. "I'm Only Sleeping"

18 Identify the Beatles song on which John Lennon blows bubbles into water, and a much-

traveled Beatle insider rattles chains inside a
bathtub.

A. "Octopus's Garden"
B. "Yellow Submarine"
C. "Lady Madonna"

19 During one memorable Beatles song, we hear
a large "audience" laugh at a visual joke of
some kind that's never explained to the listeners at home. What's the tune?

A. "Being For The Benefit Of Mr. Kite!"
B. "Mr. Moonlight"
C. "Sgt. Pepper's Lonely Hearts Club Band"

20 Which two Beatles songs are linked together
by the sound of chimes and crickets?

21 As it appears on the CD *Past Masters Volume
Two*, this song begins with the sound of birds
flying. Which is it?

A. "Hey Jude"
B. "You Know My Name (Look Up The
Number)"
C. "Across The Universe"

22 A Beatles song begins with the scratchy, distant
sound of an old-time 78 r.p.m. recording.
Which is it?

A. "Your Mother Should Know"
B. "When I'm Sixty-Four"
C. "Honey Pie"

23 This song, the first on the double-disc set *The
Beatles,* opens with the sound of a screaming jet
airliner. Name it.

24 John Lennon supposedly wanted a particular track on *Sgt. Pepper's Lonely Hearts Club Band* to conclude with a sound-parade of animals, each of which was capable of devouring the one that had just appeared. The animals are there, all right, but the appearance, near the end of the parade, of a herd of sheep—unlikely to devour any of their neighbors—indicates that his initial idea was watered down somewhat. Name the song in question, and, for extra credit, identify what the cat (early on in the parade) and the chicken (at the very end) turn into before your very ears.

25 This George Harrison track from the two-disc set *The Beatles* incorporates a bit of serendipitous rattling from a bottle of Blue Nun wine that happened to have been left on top of an amplifier. Harrison thought it sounded cool and left it in. Name the song.

A. "Long Long Long"
B. "Savoy Truffle"
C. "While My Guitar Gently Weeps"

26 This Paul McCartney composition includes the sound of a warbling bird.

A. "Blackbird"
B. "Paperback Writer"
C. "Penny Lane"

Answers

16 a) "Maxwell's Silver Hammer"

17 a) "A Day In The Life"

18 b) "Yellow Submarine." The insider was chauffeur Alf Bicknell.

19 c) "Sgt. Pepper's Lonely Hearts Club Band"

20 "You Never Give Me Your Money" and "Sun King"

21 c) "Across The Universe"

22 c) "Honey Pie"

23 "Back In The U.S.S.R."

24 The song is "Good Morning Good Morning." The two startling transformations allow the cat to turn into a dog, and the chicken to turn into an electric guitar!

25 a) "Long Long Long"

26 a) "Blackbird"

three
1962

Ready to take on some questions from the year the Beatles started to make some serious waves in Britain? (Answers begin on page 14.)

27 On New Year's Day, 1962, the Beatles auditioned for Decca Records. Among the songs they recorded that day was a cover of Motown founder Berry Gordy's very first hit as a songwriter. The number eventually showed up on the album *With The Beatles*. What song was it?

    A. "Money (That's What I Want)"
    B. "Ain't No Mountain High Enough"
    C. "Reflections"

28 A Decca executive turned down the Beatles when they auditioned for him in January of 1962—and insisted to Brian Epstein that guitar groups were on the way out. Who was he?

    A. Dick Rowe
    B. Allan Klein
    C. Derek Taylor

29 Clad in leather jackets and looking distinctly nonplused, the Beatles appeared on the front page of the January 4, 1962, *Mersey Beat*, thanks to their victory in a Liverpool popularity contest. One member of the group had his name misspelled by the paper in the caption beneath the photo. Who was it, and how did his name appear?

30 Manager Brian Epstein made a habit of assuring skeptical recording executives that the Beatles would some day be bigger than a particular American rock artist. Name him.

31 An American musician who performed on the same bill with the Beatles in 1962, and who is, at this writing, still active musically, is credited with inspiring John Lennon's early style on the harmonica. Can you name him? (Hint: Regular listeners to radio talk-show host Don Imus' syndicated morning program enjoy frequent samples of this country and western artist's fine work.)

32 Name the Liverpool club that became virtually synonymous with the Beatles in the early sixties. (Hint: It is featured prominently in the 1995 "Free As A Bird" video.)

33 True or false: On January 17, 1962, Bertrand Russell attended a Beatles performance in Liverpool, and posed for a photograph with the soon-to-be-world-famous lads that now hangs in Paul McCartney's home.

34 On May 9, 1962, Brian Epstein sent enthusiastic telegrams to the Beatles ("Congratulations boys. EMI request recording session. Please rehearse new material") and the newspaper *Mersey Beat* ("Have secured contract for Beatles to record for EMI on Parlophone label"). What crucial piece of information did Epstein withhold in these two telegrams?

A. The Beatles would be playing as backup musicians for another artist.
B. The contracts he had "secured" had not been signed, and the upcoming session was an audition.
C. Drummer Pete Best would not be taking part in the sessions because Ringo Starr had joined the group.

35 What was the date of the Beatles' first studio session at EMI?

A. January 3, 1962
B. June 6, 1962
C. December 13, 1962

36 In an interview with author Mark Hertsgaard, Apple insider Derek Taylor remarked, "If the Beatles hadn't found [him], they would have had to invent him—find some poor bastard who wasn't as good and whip him into shape." Who was Taylor referring to?

A. Drummer Ringo Starr
B. Producer George Martin
C. Engineer Geoff Emerick
D. Manager Brian Epstein

37 The Beatles performed a song at their first EMI session that showed up in the film (but not on the album) *Let It Be.* What song was it?

A. "Besame Mucho"
B. "Maggie Mae"
C. "Octopus's Garden"

38 Of what band was Ringo Starr a member before he joined the Beatles on a full-time basis?

A. Rory Storm and the Hurricanes
B. Gerry and the Pacemakers
C. Oasis

39 There are two songs in the Beatles catalog to which session drummer Andy White made a contribution. Which of these were they?

A. "Love Me Do" and "P.S. I Love You"
B. "Please Please Me" and "Misery"
C. "Anna" and "Chains"

40 True or false: Paul McCartney's name was misspelled on advance pressings of the Beatles' first single.

41 Upon meeting the Beatles for the first time, producer George Martin assured the group that they could feel comfortable telling him about anything they didn't like. What did George Harrison inform Martin that he, Harrison, didn't like?

A. His attitude
B. His tie
C. His habit of setting studio ashtrays on fire and running around the room with them on his head

42 How many Beatles could read music at the time of their signing on with EMI?

    A. Three
    B. Two
    C. None

43 What was the working title of "I Saw Her Standing There"—the title by which the Beatles referred to the number on stage during their late-1962 stage appearances?

    A. "Seventeen"
    B. "One Two Three *Faaaaw*"
    C. "Jailbait"

44 True or false: The Beatles' first British single, "Love Me Do," went to #1 on the UK charts.

45 True or false: Brian Epstein's voice can be faintly heard in the background near the end of the single release of "Love Me Do."

Answers

27 a) "Money (That's What I Want)"

28 a) Dick Rowe

29 Paul McCartney, whose last name was given as "McArtrey."

30 Elvis Presley

31 Delbert McClinton

32 The Cavern Club

33 False

34 b) The upcoming recording session was an audition, not a formal recording session for a commercial release. Epstein had in fact "secured" a contract, but it was legally unenforceable, as no representative of EMI had signed it!

35 b) June 6, 1962

36 b) Producer George Martin

37 a) "Besame Mucho"

38 a) Rory Storm and the Hurricanes

39 a) "Love Me Do" and "P.S. I Love You"

40 True; coauthorship credit was ascribed to one "Paul McArtney." Paul couldn't buy a break in those days when it came to getting his name spelled right.

41 b) Martin's tie

42 c) None of them. The members of the band, who had a habit of humming parts to Martin for him to arrange for outside artists, were not, shall we say, particularly well schooled in formal music theory.

43 a) "Seventeen"

44 False

45 False

four
BEATLE TALK

Each of the remarks below was publicly uttered by John Lennon, Paul McCartney, George Harrison, or Ringo Starr between the years 1962 and 1970. Who said what? (Answers begin on page 19.)

46 "[LSD] went on for years. I must have had a thousand trips. I used to just eat it all the time."

47 "There's high, and there's high, and to get really high—I mean so high that you can walk on the water, that high—that's where I'm goin'."

48 "I hope the fans will take up meditation instead of drugs."

49 "He's a nice fellow. We're just not going out with him anymore."

50 "Oh, it was a room and a car and a car and a room and a room and a car."

51 "Will the people in the cheaper seats clap your hands? And the rest of you, if you'll just rattle your jewelry."

52 In response to a question about whether or not he had ever dated a fan: "Yes, I have done, honestly. What more can I say?"

53 "We want to set up a system whereby people who just want to make a film about anything don't have to go on their knees in somebody's office, probably yours."

54 "I am alive and well and unconcerned about the rumors of my death. But if I were dead, I would be the last to know."

55 "When we found them [the envelopes containing notices regarding MBE medals], we thought we were being called up for the army, and then we opened them and found out we weren't."

56 "It [LSD] opened my eyes. We only use one-tenth of our brain. Just think of what we could accomplish if we could only tap that hidden part! It would mean a whole new world if the politicians would take LSD. There wouldn't be any more war or poverty or famine."

57 "I now realize that taking drugs was like taking an aspirin without having a headache."

58 "Okay, well, I don't mind. I'll play, you know, whatever you want me to play. Or I won't play at all if you don't want me to play. You know, I'm, whatever it is that will please you, I'll do it."

59 In response to the "Paul Is Dead" hysteria: "I'm not going to say anything because nobody believes me when I do."

60 "Money's got nothing to do with us... We pay tax, but we don't know how much we've made, because if we worried about that, we'd be nervous wrecks."

61 "The bank was *there,* and *that* was where the tram sheds were, and people waiting, and the inspectors stood *there,* the fire engines were down *there.* It was just reliving childhood."

62 "There's a woman in the United States who predicted the plane we were traveling on would crash. Now, a lot of people would like to think we were scared into saying a prayer. What we did actually—we drank."

63 "Christianity will go. It will vanish and shrink. I needn't argue about that. I'm right and will be proved right. We're more popular than Jesus now; I don't know which will go first, rock 'n' roll or Christianity. Jesus was all right, but his disciples were thick and ordinary. It's them twisting it that ruins it for me."

64 "Look, I wasn't saying the Beatles are better than God or Jesus. I said 'Beatles' because it's easy for me to talk about Beatles. I could have said TV or the cinema, motor cars or anything popular and I would have gotten away with it."

65 In response to the question "Do you feel you are being crucified?": "No, I wouldn't say that at all."

66 "We never write anything with themes. We just write the same rubbish all the time."

67 "When two great Saints meet, it is a humbling experience."

68 "When you're drowning, you don't say 'I would be incredibly pleased if someone would have the foresight to notice me drowning and come and help me,' you just *scream*."

69 Explaining the motives behind the breakup of the Beatles: "Personal differences, musical differences, business differences, but most of all because I have a better time with my family."

70 "I'm a tidy sort of bloke. I don't like chaos. I kept records in the record rack, tea in the tea caddy, and pot in the pot box."

71 "We're thinking it might be nice if we conceive [a child] in Amsterdam. We might call it 'Amsterdam' or 'Peace' or 'Hair' or 'Bed-In' or something. It would be beautiful."

72 "Us, communists? Why, we can't be communists. We're the world's number one capitalists. Imagine us communists!"

73 "I'd like to end up sort of unforgettable."

74 "I think the French girls are fabulous."

Answers

46 John Lennon, 1970

47 George Harrison, circa 1968

48 Ringo Starr, 1967

49 Paul McCartney, 1968, referring to Maharishi

Mahesh Yogi.

50 John Lennon, 1963. The remark was eventually incorporated in the film *A Hard Day's Night*.

51 John Lennon, 1963. The joke was a high point of the group's set during the Royal Variety Performance before members of the British Royal Family.

52 John Lennon, 1964

53 John Lennon, 1968

54 Paul McCartney, 1969

55 George Harrison, 1965

56 Paul McCartney, 1967

57 Paul McCartney, 1967

58 George Harrison, 1969

59 Ringo Starr, circa 1969

60 George Harrison, 1966

61 John Lennon, 1970. He is discussing the song "Penny Lane," a Paul McCartney composition.

62 Ringo Starr, 1966

63 John Lennon, 1966

64 John Lennon, 1966

65 John Lennon, 1966

66 John Lennon, 1964

67 Paul McCartney, 1969. The remark appears on the infamous *Two Virgins* LP.

68 John Lennon, 1970

69 Paul McCartney, 1970

70 George Harrison, 1969

71 John Lennon, 1969

72 Paul McCartney, 1966

73 Ringo Starr, 1964

74 Paul McCartney, 1963

five
1963

England falls in love with the Beatles big time. How many of the following questions about the year 1963 can you answer? (Answers begin on page 27.)

75 True or false: The Beatles' early recordings featured the songwriting credit "McCartney/Lennon," rather than "Lennon/McCartney," on the label.

76 On what program did the Beatles make their first national broadcast appearance in England?

    A. "Meet the Wife"
    B. "Thank Your Lucky Stars"
    C. "That Was the Week That Was"

77 Shortly after the Beatles had experienced modest British chart success with their first single, George Martin encouraged the group to record a number that had been written by an established songwriter. They laid down the track, but opted instead to release an up-tempo

version of a previously rejected Lennon/
McCartney tune. What song did the Beatles
record at Martin's behest—and leave officially unreleased until 1995's *The Beatles
Anthology 1?*

A. "How Do You Do It?"
B. "Crazy"
C. "The Girl From Ipanema"

78 What band, also managed by Brian Epstein,
released a version of this song instead of the
Beatles—and took it to the top of the British
charts?

79 The Beatles engaged in a marathon one-day
session in which they recorded ten of the
fourteen tracks for their first LP, *Please Please
Me.* (Four songs from two previously released
singles made up the rest of the record.) What
was the date of this landmark rock 'n' roll
workday?

A. April 23, 1963
B. February 11, 1963
C. March 12, 1963

80 This day's work was all the more remarkable in
that it featured a thirteen-take attempt to
record a song that never showed up on the
album *Please Please Me.* What song was it?

A. "Hold Me Tight"
B. "I Am The Walrus"
C. "Ticket To Ride"

81 On their first LP, the Beatles covered a song

released by the American group the Cookies. What was the song—and who wrote it?

82 True or false: Nudism/pop pioneer John Lennon recorded "Twist And Shout" shirtless.

83 True or false: "Twist And Shout" was the first song undertaken during the one-day session when most of the songs for the Beatles' first LP were recorded.

84 How many takes were required for the Beatles' final version of "Twist And Shout"?

85 Who had scored an American hit with "Twist And Shout" *before* the Beatles covered the tune on their first LP?

A. The Chambers Brothers
B. The Righteous Brothers
C. The Isley Brothers

86 The song "Do You Want To Know A Secret," which appears on the Beatles' first LP, was inspired by a tune from a Walt Disney picture that Julia Lennon used to sing her son John. Identify it.

A. "Whistle While You Work"
B. "Wishing Well"
C. "A Whole New World"

87 What was the first released Beatles song to boast a Ringo Starr vocal?

A. "Honey Don't"
B. "What Goes On"
C. "Boys"

88 What title did producer George Martin suggest for the first Beatles LP?

    A. *The Beige Album*
    B. *Off The Beatle Track*
    C. *Four By Four*

89 Name the on-the-spot composition Messrs. Lennon and McCartney handed over to the Messrs. Jagger and Richards, thus helping the Rolling Stones to score an important early hit.

    A. "Sympathy For The Devil"
    B. "You'd Better Move On"
    C. "I Wanna Be Your Man"

90 The album *Please Please Me* reached the top of the UK LP charts in May of 1963 for a long reign as the nation's top seller. What competing album finally took over the #1 spot from *Please Please Me* near the end of 1963?

91 The Beatles wrote one of their biggest hits while on a bus—during a time when the band was on tour with the singer Helen Shapiro. The song in question topped the British charts for seven weeks in 1963. Can you name it?

    A. "From Me To You"
    B. "Please Please Me"
    C. "I Saw Her Standing There"

92 True or false: The term "Beatlemania" was first coined in 1963 by John Lennon.

93 What was the name of the Beatles' radio show on the BBC?

94 Can you name the first Beatles composition to be recorded by another artist?

95 What remarkable pop-chart claim to fame does the Beatles' "She Love You" hold in the United Kingdom?

96 The single "She Loves You" was released in Britain to thunderous success in 1963, but manager Brian Epstein couldn't convince Capitol Records to take the song on for release in the United States. Even the unassuming Vee Jay label, which had earlier released the LP *Introducing The Beatles* to the American market with no notable success, took a pass. Can you name the label Epstein did cajole into handling the single, which was destined to become a #1 hit in the States the following year?

97 True or false: In late 1963, desperate to crack the American market, the Beatles recorded, but decided not to release, a song expressing Britain's appreciation for American humanitarian and military assistance during World War II.

98 What was George Harrison's first solo composition to appear on a Beatles album?

99 While recording the LP *With The Beatles*, George Harrison handled the lead vocal on a Chuck Berry number that John Lennon had previously sung in the group's stage act. What was the song?

100 True or false: The liner notes for the album *With The Beatles* misidentify the title of "It Won't Be Long."

101 What country did the Beatles visit for their first-ever foreign tour?

102 What major world news event took place on the day that *With The Beatles* was released in the United Kingdom?

103 True or false: The album *With The Beatles* debuted at #1 in the UK charts.

104 What was the Beatles' last #1 single of the year 1963 in Britain?

105 At what position did this single debut on the UK charts?

Answers

75 True. The "McCartney/Lennon" approach stuck for the group's earliest compositions; the first to be issued under the familiar "Lennon/ McCartney" credit was "She Loves You."

76 b) ITV's "Thank Your Lucky Stars," on January 19, 1963

77 a) "How Do You Do It?" The song they released instead: "Please Please Me."

78 Gerry and the Pacemakers turned it into their first #1 hit.

79 b) February 11, 1963

80 a) "Hold Me Tight." It eventually showed up on *With The Beatles* in the UK, and on *Meet The Beatles!* in the U.S.

81 The song was "Chains." It was written by

Gerry Goffin and Carole King, two standouts of the fabled Brill Building stable of writers.

82 True

83 False. It was the last piece of work of a *very* long day; Lennon's exhausted voice can be heard deteriorating magnificently as the song progresses. Never have frayed vocal cords been put to better service.

84 The electrifying version that appears on the record is, amazingly, the group's very first take. A second one was laid down, but Lennon's voice was shot by that time.

85 c) The Isley Brothers

86 b) "Wishing Well," from *Snow White and the Seven Dwarfs*

87 c) "Boys"

88 b) *Off The Beatle Track*. The record was, of course, eventually titled *Please Please Me*, but Martin used *Off The Beatle Track* as the title of a later album of orchestral arrangements of Beatle tunes.

89 c) "I Wanna Be Your Man"

90 *With The Beatles*. Mind-boggling as it may seem, the Beatles released their new album while the previous entry was still perched at the top of the British charts! Well, it *was* the holiday season. *Please Please Me* occupied the top position in the UK album charts for twenty-nine consecutive weeks before yielding to *With The Beatles*, which had a similarly sur-realistic stretch at the top. Altogether, the

Beatles had the best-selling album in Britain for very nearly one solid year.

91 a) "From Me To You"

92 False. It was the creation of British newspaper editors during that year.

93 "Pop Go the Beatles"

94 "Misery," which was covered by Kenny Lynch

95 It reached the #1 position on two separate occasions—September 12, 1963, for four weeks, and November 28, 1963, for two weeks!

96 Swan Records

97 False

98 "Don't Bother Me," which appeared on *With the Beatles* in the UK and *Meet the Beatles!* in the U.S.

99 "Roll Over, Beethoven"

100 True. The offending passage, which refers to the track as "It Won't Be Long Now," can be found on page 6 of the current CD release's booklet.

101 Sweden; they left October 24, 1963.

102 American President John F. Kennedy was assassinated; the date, of course, was November 22, 1963.

103 True

104 "I Want To Hold Your Hand"

105 Number one

six

Studio Stuff

ow deep is your knowledge of the Beatles' studio technique? Give the following questions a try. Ready? And . . . take one . . . (Answers begin on page 34.)

106 In a bit of studio magic still discussed reverently by Beatles fans, George Martin fused two different takes of "Strawberry Fields Forever," despite the fact that they differed in both tempo and key, to yield the finished version of the song with which we are familiar today. Where does the edit occur in the song?

107 How much total studio time—excluding breaks—did the Beatles require to complete the ten new songs on their first album?

    A. Nine hours and forty-five minutes
    B. Twelve hours and fifteen minutes
    C. Fourteen hours and thirty minutes

108 How much studio time did the Beatles require to complete the songs on *Sgt. Pepper's Lonely Hearts Club Band?*

    A. One month
    B. Three months
    C. Five months

109 What do the following songs have in common: "Eleanor Rigby," "The Inner Light," and "Good Night"?

110 The year 1965 marked a studio milestone for the group: on one of the tracks released that year, the Beatles appealed, for the first time, to an outside studio musician (other than producer George Martin, or drummer Andy White, who contributed to some very early sessions). Name the song and the instrument in question.

111 In his fine book *A Day In The Life,* author Mark Hertsgaard writes that, in orchestrating and editing a particular Beatles track, producer George Martin "does such an uncanny job of expressing the drug experience that one is almost tempted to doubt his assurances that he never tried LSD." What song is Hertsgaard discussing?

112 In 1970, producer Phil Spector was given the challenging assignment of turning the *Get Back* tapes and related tracks into a listenable soundtrack album to accompany the release of the film *Let It Be.* One of the dilemmas facing Spector was a number entitled "I Me Mine," a track that represents the Beatles' very last studio effort as something vaguely resembling a group. The version before him had been recorded long after the filming of the movie (and, indeed, after the sessions for *Abbey Road*) by Paul McCartney, Ringo Starr, and George Harrison—John Lennon being abroad at the time. But the "finished" version of the song presented to Spector ran only 1:34 in length, a bit brisk for an LP that needed every full-length track it could get. By the time he set to work on the track, the prospect of reassembling the group for another round of studio work was a nonstarter. How did Spector end up delivering a track of 2:25 duration without access to any Beatles?

113 By early 1967, the Beatles had finished work on a song that had consumed fifty-five hours of studio time, a far cry indeed from the breakneck pace of the *Please Please Me* album. Identify the song that was the object of this remarkable amount of attention.

A. "A Day In The Life"
B. "Strawberry Fields Forever"
C. "Penny Lane"

114 Paul McCartney instructed a studio engineer named John Kurlander to throw away a bit of music he had once thought could go directly after "Mean Mr. Mustard" on the extended *Abbey Road* Side Two medley. Instead of doing so, Kurlander spliced the fragment onto the end of a spool of tape bearing the rest of the medley. The result: McCartney played the tape later and was startled to hear, after a protracted silence, the thunderous chord deleted from the end of "Mean Mr. Mustard"—and the tongue-in-cheek ditty that would eventually appear as the final track on *Abbey Road*. Name the song in question—and, for extra credit, explain why its final note is missing.

115 To achieve just the right vocal track for a particular song on *The Beatles*, John Lennon recorded it while lying flat on the floor of the Abbey Road studios. What song was it?

A. "Revolution 1"
B. "Yer Blues"
C. "Everybody's Got Something To Hide Except Me And My Monkey"

116 What was the first Beatles album to feature a Moog synthesizer?

A. *The Beatles*
B. *Abbey Road*
C. *Let It Be*

117 Excluding the reunion songs recorded by Messrs. Harrison, McCartney, and Starr in the nineties, name the only officially released Beatles recording on which studio work *began* after January 1, 1970.

A. "Two Of Us"
B. "Come Together"
C. "I Me Mine"

118 The surviving Beatles took a good deal of heat from some quarters for pressing John Lennon's demo recordings into service for their nineties reunion songs "Free As A Bird" and "Real

Love." One of the Beatles' own #1 singles, however, is also based on a very shaky bit of initial recording, later spruced up by its producer for a mainstream release. What song was it?

A. "The Long And Winding Road"
B. "Get Back"
C. "Lady Madonna"

119 Many fans of John Lennon's noticed that his vocal on the "Real Love" track has an unusually "Beatle-ish" sound for a track whose origin is a tape Lennon made in the late seventies. Part of this effect can be accounted for by the decision to speed the vocal track up a notch—but not all of it. A nineties production choice helped to render Lennon's vocal uncannily evocative of pre-1970 Beatles output. What was it?

A. Overdubbing of 1967 Lennon vocal tapes
B. A Paul McCartney vocal track
C. Séances in the studio

Answers

106 At approximately 1:00. To hear it most clearly, listen to only the left channel of the song through a pair of headphones. Around the phrase "going to . . ." you'll hear a sudden shift in the tone of Lennon's vocal, as well as an unexpected change in the drum track.

107 a) Nine hours and forty-five minutes, all clocked on one extraordinary day: February 11, 1963.

108 c) Approximately five months. The sessions began in late November of 1966 and did not conclude until April of 1967.

109 The Beatles supplied only vocal tracks and made no instrumental contribution whatsoever to these songs. There is one other track that fits this description; it appears on the *Sgt. Pepper* album. Any guesses? If you can't come up with the answer, see question #363.

110 The song: "You've Got to Hide Your Love Away." The instrument: the flute, played by Johnnie Scott.

111 "Strawberry Fields Forever"

112 By repeating a significant chunk of it. The edit, which long eluded many Beatles fans—including this one—occurs at around 1:21 of the song. It is referenced in Mark Lewisohn's *The Beatles: Recording Sessions*.

113 b) "Strawberry Fields Forever"

114 "Her Majesty." When Kurlander removed the song from the medley, its final note was accidentally lopped off.

115 a) "Revolution 1"

116 b) *Abbey Road*

117 c) "I Me Mine." The 1969 performance of this song that appears in the film *Let It Be* is, from a recording point of view at any rate, unrelated to the studio track that appears on the album.

118 a) "The Long And Winding Road," Phil Spector's syrupy reworking of which was the cause of much intense discussion during the band's 1970 public-breakup phase. The track was based on some instrumentally thin taped material from the January 1969 *Get Back* sessions; it turned out to be the Beatles' final #1 single in the United States.

119 b) Poor recording quality on the basic vocal track made it necessary for Paul McCartney to sing an accompanying vocal—not for purposes of harmony, but simply to fill in, via modern high-tech means, the holes in the original. The result is a predominantly "Lennon" vocal seamlessly bonded with occasional "McCartney" overtones!

seven

1964

America goes nuts for the Fab Four. What's your B.Q. (Beatle Quotient) for the fateful year 1964? (Answers begin on page 50.)

120 What was the Beatles' first #1 single in the United States?

121 In January of 1964, the Beatles recorded German-language versions of two of their songs. In what city did they do this?

   A. Hamburg
   B. West Berlin
   C. Paris

122 Can you provide the English *and* German titles of the songs in question?

123 "She Loves You" was a smash hit in the United States in 1964; in fact, according to a 1976 list printed by *Billboard* magazine, it was one of the group's two biggest-ever singles in America.

What Beatles single topped "She Loves You" in the Stateside popularity sweepstakes?

A. "Help!"
B. "Hey Jude"
C. "Let It Be"

1964: THE EXPERTS SPEAK

In America, the onset of Beatlemania was a confusing time. . . for grownups. Good thing plenty of commentators were around to help make sense of things, eh? One of the quotes below is fictitious. Your job is to spot it—and attribute the rest to the following esteemed personages and/or institutions: William F. Buckley, Jr.; Chet Huntley; Dr. Joyce Brothers; The Reverend Dr. Billy Graham; *Variety* magazine.

124 "[The Beatles'] 'Oliver' haircuts and too-short jackets are part of the. . . fanciful mystique. (The Dickens hero) Oliver Twist, you will recall, was an orphan. By embracing a quartet of orphans as heroes, our teenagers. . . symbolically 'kill off' the adult generation."

125 "The Beatles—they're a passing phase, symptoms of the uncertainty of the times and the confusion about us."

126 "Like a good little news organization, we sent three cameramen out to Kennedy airport today to cover the arrival of a group from England known as the Beatles. . . I feel there is absolutely no need to show any of that film."

127 "My personal view is that the music is not particularly audible, the sentiments are not particularly original, and the hair is not particularly clean. Beyond that, I suppose they're nice enough as long as they aren't Marxists."

128 "[Beatlemania may be] closely linked to the current wave of racial rioting."

129 "[Beatlemania is] like a sickness, which is not a cultivated hallucinatory weakness, but something that derives from a lamentable and organic imbalance. . . . What then, gods and goddesses, was our sin. . . ? We may not know what it was, even as Oedipus did not know, during all those years, the reasons why he was cursed."

———

130 True or false: The Beatles were in Liverpool when they first learned that they had hit the #1 spot on the American charts.

131 Admit it: You never did understand all the words to "Long Tall Sally." Or did you? Supply the phrase that precedes the line about Sally having everything Uncle John needs.

132 During their first American press conference, Paul McCartney gave a direct answer to a reporter's question concerning the Beatles' "message" to the United States. What was it?

133 Before the Beatles appeared live on the "Ed Sullivan Show," another American TV personality featured film of the group on his show. Name him.

134 The-show-must-go-on department: Identify

the Beatle who checked in for the all-impor-
tant February 9, 1964, "Ed Sullivan Show"
appearance despite having come down with
the flu.

135 How many separate broadcasts of the "Ed
Sullivan Show" featured the Beatles during
February 1964?

A. One
B. Two
C. Three

136 On April 4, 1964, the Beatles steamrolled over
the competition on the *Billboard* Hot Hundred
list, occupying not just the #1 position in the
U.S., but the next four slots as well. Can you
name the five hottest songs in America that
week—without consulting the *Guinness Book
of World Records*?

137 During the first few months of Beatlemania in
the U.S., it seemed that virtually any record
with the word "Beatles" attached to it could sell
in impressive quantities. Name the Hamburg-
era cover tune with a lead vocal by John
Lennon, fashioned by Atco Records into a
"new" Beatles single, that cracked the American
Top Twenty during this period.

A. "Ain't She Sweet"
B. "My Bonnie"
C. "Whole Lotta Lonely"

138 The first *non-Beatle* song, recorded in England
by an English act, to reach the #1 spot in the

United States was a Lennon/McCartney composition. Name it.

A. "A World Without Love"
B. "That Means A Lot"
C. "Come And Get It"

1964: THE FANZINES SPEAK

Get ready for some excerpts of text from various fan publications focusing on the Beatles, circa 1964. Read the passages below. Some are genuine. Some are not. Your job: determine which is which.

139 John Lennon's personal ambition: "To write musical."

140 Paul McCartney's personal ambition: "To meet Bridget Bardot."

141 George Harrison's personal ambition: "To design a guitar."

142 Ringo Starr's personal ambition: "To own a line of manicure salons."

143 From an article entitled "How To Dance The Beatle!": "Standing side by side, bend from the hips and shake your shoulders. Put right hand behind head and wiggle your fingers."

144 "Yes, you can actually win a phone call from The Beatles! That is the fantastic first prize in this super-fabulous contest! . . . Simply tell, in 50 words or less, just why you want to talk to The Beatles! Easy, isn't it? Then stand by your phone, and soon you might just hear the groovy English accents of this fabulous group!"

145 "John Lennon? Married? He really knows how to hurt a girl, doesn't he? As though we'd settle for one of the other three!"

146 "The Beatles have arrived! They took England by storm, but then, they came from England, so they really had a head start."

147 From an excerpt of George Harrison's "hates and loves": "I hate having to hurry past a crowd of fans without stopping for a chat."

148 "If Ringo were elected President, could he legally serve out his term of office? The experts speak!"

149 "Jane Asher Color Pic! See What She Really Looks Like!"

150 John Lennon's "favorite band": Quincy Jones.

151 From an article entitled "A Psychiatrist Looks At Beatlemania": "Dixon Scott of the London *Daily Mirror* interviewed a well-known psychiatrist (unnamed because of professional ethics) in an attempt to get at the root of Beatlemania. 'We are all chaotic and mixed-up inside,' the psychiatrist told Scott."

152 Among "Instruments played" by Ringo Starr: "Guitar."

═══════

153 What was the name of the Beatles' licensing organization?

154 American Beatles fans with no access to the import bins had to wait for the release of *Past Masters: Volume One* to own a "clean" version of a certain 1964 Beatles rocker. The U.S. version of the song in question had, for some reason, been layered over with gobs of echo. Can you name the tune?

155 On the floor of the House of Commons in 1964, John Lennon's literary merits were addressed by one Charles Curran, who suggested that the Beatle author had "picked up bits of Tennyson, Browning, and Robert Louis Stevenson while listening with one ear to the football results on the wireless." Curran also opined that Lennon's writings exhibited a "pathetic state of near-literacy." Can you identify the publication of Lennon's that sent Curran off the deep end?

  A. *In His Own Write*
  B. *A Spaniard In The Works*
  C. *Why Christianity Will Fail*

156 In March of 1964, John Lennon's first book appeared; many reviews cited parallels between the author's free-form literary style and that of James Joyce. One of the passages that follows is from Joyce's *Finnegan's Wake;* the other is from Lennon's work. Which is which?

  A. "All the vitalmines is beginning to sozzle in chewn, fudgem, kates and epas and naboc and erics and oinnos on kingclud. . . "
  B. "Amo amat amass; amonk amink aminibus. Amarmyladie Moon; amikky

mendip multiplus amighty midgey
spoon. . . "

157 Those in attendance at the Foyle's Literary
Luncheon given in author John Lennon's
honor probably had no difficulty memorizing
the entire text of the speech he gave on that
occasion. How much of it can you recite?

158 How did George Harrison meet his future
wife Patti Boyd?

A. She was a stewardess on a plane flight the
   Beatles chartered.
B. She had a small role in the film *A Hard
   Day's Night*.
C. She followed the group's limousine for a
   mile and a half until Harrison instructed
   the driver to let her in.

159 How long did it take American record-buyers
to snatch up a quarter of a million copies of
the single "I Want To Hold Your Hand" when
it was first released?

A. Two days
B. Three days
C. Four days

160 Since the U.S. release of the Beatles' authoritative British CD catalog, the patchwork
American LP *Meet The Beatles!* has become a
distant memory, even a collector's item. It was,
nevertheless, one of the most popular records
in American history, which leads one to the
natural question: What songs appeared on it?

161 In 1964 Capitol Records released *The Beatles' Second Album*. Alert fans quickly spotted a technical error on the cover. What was it?

162 How many of the tracks appearing on the Beatles' 1964 American LP release *Something New* were in fact Lennon/McCartney compositions entirely new to the American market?

   A. Four
   B. Three
   C. Two

163 True or false: In 1964, the Beatles released a double-album set with the Dave Clark Five.

164 True or false: In 1964, the Beatles released a double-album set with the Four Seasons.

165 At 1:25 of the song "She's A Woman," something funny happens to the insistent, repetitive rhythm guitar riff. What?

166 True or false: In 1964, the recently hospitalized Ringo Starr sold his glass-encased tonsils to an anonymous Amsterdam bidder for $37,500.

167 A question for the guitar players in the audience: Can you identify the unmistakable opening chord of the song "A Hard Day's Night"?

1964: A HARD DAY'S NIGHT

Although the snootier film critics routinely exclude the film from their ten-best-of-all-time lists, few of them could name many movies that are more fun than the Fabs' first cinema release.

Herewith some questions about history's most satisfying rock 'n' roll picture.

168 Why doesn't the song "A Hard Day's Night" appear as one of the numbers the Beatles perform during the television appearance that serves as the highlight of the film?

169 Name all the Beatles songs that can be heard during the film *A Hard Day's Night*.

170 What is the name of the Beatles' manager in the film?

171 What is the name of the manager's assistant—the fellow who obstinately insists on being taller than is seemly?

172 Which Beatle is asked, during an encounter with the press in *A Hard Day's Night,* whether or not success has changed his life? What is his answer?

173 What request does John Lennon make when informed that the immediate surroundings are surging with girls?

174 What does George Harrison call his hairstyle during *A Hard Day's Night*?

175 What song do we hear as the Beatles cavort in an open field?

176 Which Beatle, after being upbraided about trespassing on private property, responds with the immortal line "Sorry if we hurt your field, Mister"?

177 Shades of "Star Trek"! Complete this line of Ringo's from *A Hard Day's Night*. "I'm a drummer, not a. . . "

178 Who plays Paul McCartney's fictional grandfather in *A Hard Day's Night?*

179 What is Paul's fictional grandfather's first name?

180 During a conversation in the commissary, Ringo is informed that there is something better than books. What is it?

181 Ringo Starr's melancholy demeanor during the "walk-by-the-canal" portion of *A Hard Day's Night* earned him much critical praise. When the televised documentary *The Beatles Anthology* was broadcast in 1995, Beatle fans learned the real source of the "emotions" on display during this sequence. What was it?

182 During his walk in this part of the film, Starr meets up with a young boy who, like the drummer, is on temporary leave from his mates. What is the youngster's name?

A. Charlie
B. Pete
C. Stu

183 Starr is eventually hauled into a London police station on charges of "wandering abroad," "malicious intent," "acting in a suspicious manner," and "conduct liable to cause a breach of the peace." What fellow-rebel does he meet in the station?

184 Name the songs the Beatles perform during the televised performance that is the climax of the film *A Hard Day's Night*.

185 While the Beatles are performing on the live television broadcast, Paul's grandfather rises up through the stage floor. Which Beatle tosses him offstage?

186 True or false: The screenplay for *A Hard Day's Night* was nominated for an Academy Award.

——————

187 In 1964, George Harrison passed along a copy of a recent Bob Dylan album to John Lennon. The eventual result was a profound shift in Lennon's songwriting style, evidenced in numbers like "You've Got To Hide Your Love Away." Can you name the album that introduced Lennon to Dylan's work?

188 In 1964, the Beatles appeared in a television film called *Around the Beatles*, one of the highlights of which was a Fab rendition of a scene from Shakespeare. What play of the Bard's did the four lads from Liverpool liven up on this occasion?

189 The Beatles released a U.S. single that featured the first faded-in introduction in pop music history. Name the song.

190 Name the 1964 Beatles hit that fades out to the sound of someone barking like a dog.

191 True or false: During the Beatles' 1964 tour of Australia, a sound engineer reported that the noise from the crowd at a Beatles' concert exceeded that of a functioning jet engine.

192 While preparing the tracks for what was to become the Christmas-release LP *Beatles For Sale,* the Beatles recorded—but left unreleased—a superb version of a rhythm-and-blues number that had been previously recorded by Little Willie John. Name the song. (Hint: The tune was one of the highlights of 1995's *The Beatles Anthology 1*, and was much bootlegged in the decades before that compilation appeared.)

193 Jimi Hendrix fans, take note. A 1964 Beatles single featured what was, at the time, a startling pop innovation: intentionally generated guitar feedback! What song incorporated this Lennon–inspired brainstorm?

A. "She's A Woman"
B. "I Feel Fine"
C. "Eight Days A Week"

194 "Mr. Moonlight," which appears on the 1964 LP *Beatles For Sale* in Britain and on *Beatles '65* in the U.S., is regarded by many Beatles fans as the single cheesiest track the group ever laid down. Who released the song originally?

A. James Brown
B. Carl Perkins
C. Dr. Feelgood and the Interns

195 What unusual percussion "instrument" does Ringo Starr add to the Beatles' cover of the Buddy Holly number "Words Of Love" on the LP *Beatles For Sale*?

196 The Beatles won two Grammys in 1964. For what categories did they win?

197 True or false: While vacationing in the Philippines in 1964, Ringo Starr took time to do a special promotional film with Imelda

Marcos encouraging British investment in Filipino industry.

198 During 1964 in the United States, it seemed as if there were no article of clothing, confection, school supply item, magazine, or hairstyle that was incapable of being marketed with a Beatle tie-in. What 1968 film initiated the *second* massive Beatles merchandising blitz?

199 What was the Beatles' last #1 single of 1964 in the United States?

200 In 1964, the Beatles smoked marijuana for the first time. Who turned them on?

Answers

120 "I Want To Hold Your Hand"

121 c) Paris, France

122 "She Loves You"/"Sie Liebt Dich" and "I Want To Hold Your Hand"/"Komm, Gib Mir Deine Hand"

123 b) "Hey Jude"

124 Dr. Joyce Brothers

125 The Reverend Dr. Billy Graham

126 Chet Huntley, speaking on the NBC evening news of February 7, 1964.

127 This quote is fictitious.

128 *Variety*

129 William F. Buckley, Jr.

130 False: They were in Paris, France.

131 The phrase is "she's built pretty sweet," but McCartney more or less demolishes the Little Richard lyric. Sounds great, though.

132 "Buy more Beatles records."

133 Jack Paar, in January of 1964

134 George Harrison

135 c) Three. Two—February 9 and 16—were live, and one—February 23—was taped.

136 #1 "Can't Buy Me Love"; #2 "Twist And Shout"; #3 "She Loves You"; #4 "I Want To Hold Your Hand"; #5 "Please Please Me."

137 a) "Ain't She Sweet"

138 a) "A World Without Love," by Peter and Gordon

139 Genuine

140 Fictitious

141 Genuine

142 Fictitious. Actually, it was hair salons Ringo was interested in around this time.

143 Genuine

144 Genuine

145 Fictitious

146 Genuine

147 Genuine

148 Fictitious

149 Genuine

150 Genuine

151 Genuine

152 Genuine

153 Seltaeb—"Beatles" spelled backwards

154 "She's a Woman." The reverberating, overproduced American version appears on *Beatles '65*.

155 a) *In His Own Write*

156 a) is Joyce; b) is Lennon.

157 The speech in its entirety: "Thank you very much. You've got a lucky face."

158 b) She had a small role in the film *A Hard Day's Night*; the two met during filming.

159 b) Three days

160 For those of you programming your CD changers at home, the running order was as follows. Side One: "I Want To Hold Your Hand," "I Saw Her Standing There," "This Boy," "It Won't Be Long," "All I've Got To Do." Side Two: "Don't Bother Me," "Little Child," "Till There Was You," "Hold Me Tight," "I Wanna Be Your Man," "Not A Second Time."

161 The album's title. Discounting records featuring material by other artists, the American LP entitled *The Beatles' Second Album* was in fact the Beatles' *third* American album release. The other two had been *Introducing The Beatles* (released by Vee Jay, and a #2 hit on the album chart in 1964), and Capitol's *Meet The Beatles!*

162 b) Only three: "Things We Said Today," "Any Time At All," and "When I Get Home." The album consisted primarily of songs released the previous month on the American soundtrack album of *A Hard Day's Night*!

163 False

164 True—although Vee Jay Records had more to say about the release than the Beatles themselves ever did. The double album was called *The Beatles vs. The Four Seasons,* and it represented Vee Jay's last-gasp effort to cash in on its control of the tracks appearing on its earlier release *Introducing The Beatles.* One disc contained (old) Beatles music; the other, a collection of Four Seasons material. You, the listener, were meant to be the final judge as to which band was most worthy of adulation. Commerce really is the truest form of democracy, isn't it?

165 It disappears for a beat.

166 False

167 G eleventh suspended fourth.

168 The song had not been recorded in time for inclusion in the film, so "A Hard Day's Night"—the tune—was used as the background music for the opening title sequence of *A Hard Day's Night*—the movie. As though to remedy the problem, an extremely brief (and not very serious) a cappella burst of the song surfaces during a scene when the boys return to the station after looking for Ringo, but it is clearly a later vocal overdub.

169 "A Hard Day's Night," "I Should Have Known Better," "If I Fell," "I'm Happy Just To Dance With You," "And I Love Her," "Tell Me Why," "She Loves You," and "Can't Buy Me Love."

170 Norm

171 Shake

172 George Harrison; "Yes."

173 "Please sir, can I have one to surge with, sir, please, sir?"

174 Arthur

175 "Can't Buy Me Love"

176 George Harrison

177 ". . . wet nurse."

178 Wilfred Brambell

179 John

180 Parading

181 Starr was a little woozy, thanks to a lively round of partying he had not yet slept off. As any good *method* actor would, he used the grimaces and unsteady bearing resulting from his previous evening's festivities to artistic advantage.

182 a) Charlie

183 Paul's grandfather

184 "Tell Me Why," "If I Fell," "I Should Have Known Better," and "She Loves You"

185 George Harrison

186 True. Alun Owen's fine script was nominated for Best Story & Screenplay Written Directly for the Screen.

187 *The Freewheelin' Bob Dylan*

188 *A Midsummer Night's Dream*

189 "Eight Days a Week"

190 "I Feel Fine"

191 True

192 "Leave My Kitten Alone"

193 b) "I Feel Fine"

194 c) The immortal Dr. Feelgood and the Interns, in 1962. "Mr. Moonlight" served as the B side—and how—for the band's self-titled release "Dr. Feelgood."

195 A packing case

196 Best New Artist, and Best Vocal Performance by a Group (for "A Hard Day's Night").

197 False

198 *Yellow Submarine*

199 "I Feel Fine"

200 Bob Dylan

eight
THE BEATLES—LIVE!

You couldn't always *hear* them, but the Beatles' shows were generally Happenings with a capital H. Test your knowledge of the group's touring and concert history by tackling the following questions. (Answers begin on page 58.)

201 True or false: A towel used by the Beatles "to dry their faces immediately following their Hollywood Bowl concert, August 23, 1964," was cut up into small segments that were mounted on small cards and sold as souvenirs.

202 June of 1964—the height of Beatlemania—and Ringo Starr had to sit out part of a major world tour due to tonsillitis. Who took his place behind the drums until he could rejoin the group?

203 In what country did Ringo rejoin the group for the tour?

204 Identify the wealthy American businessman—and future agitator on behalf of the designated-hitter rule in American League baseball—who used a $150,000 offer to persuade the Beatles to forgo a planned day off and perform in Kansas City, Missouri in 1964.

205 What was the date of the Beatles' legendary 1965 concert at Shea Stadium?

206 Who introduced the Beatles to the crowd before their landmark 1965 appearance at Shea Stadium?

207 What inventive way of playing the electric piano did John Lennon use to inspire fits of laughter from George Harrison during the 1965 Shea Stadium concert? On what number did this incident occur?

208 True or false: While on tour in Canada, the Beatles got wind of an anti-Semitic death threat that had been made against Ringo Starr, whom the demented would-be assailant assumed (erroneously) to be Jewish.

209 John Lennon's vocal work on the legendary first-take masterpiece "Twist And Shout" has earned a spot in pop recording history, but in 1964, Paul McCartney performed a similar bit of first-take magic while covering a rock 'n' roll number that had, like "Twist And Shout," long been a staple of the group's live performances. In fact, the tune McCartney recorded holds the distinction of being the only number to have appeared more or less consistently in the group's repertoire from the early days (1957) all the way to their final concert appearance in San Francisco's Candlestick Park. Can you name the song?

210 Among several unfortunate events marring the Beatles' 1966 world tour was a stop to an Asian country where the band members' understandable desire to take advantage of a rare day off resulted in a perceived slight to the wife of the president. Name the country and the outraged First Lady.

211 On August 29, 1966, the Beatles made their final appearance before a paying audience at San Francisco's Candlestick Park. How many of the songs performed on that historic occasion were from the album *Revolver*, released three weeks earlier?

A. Five
B. Three
C. Zero

212 What was the date of the rooftop performance that serves as the unforgettable ending to *Let It Be*—and the Beatles' last live performance as a group in front of an audience?

A. January 30, 1969
B. January 30, 1970
C. April 10, 1970

Answers

201 True

202 Jimmy Nicol

203 Australia

204 Charles O. Finley

205 August 15, 1965

206 Ed Sullivan

207 Lennon played the piano with his elbow on "I'm Down." He and Harrison can be seen cracking up throughout the number on the televised documentary *The Beatles Anthology 2*.

208 True

209 "Long Tall Sally"

210 The country was the Philippines; the First Lady was Imelda Marcos, who had extended an invitation to the Beatles to visit her—one that was politely declined. When the Fabs failed to materialize, the national media provoked the populace into anti-Beatles demonstrations. The members of the band got out of the country safely—but only after having been dealt with rather roughly by some of President Marcos' representatives at the airport.

211 c) Not a one

212 January 30, 1969

nine

1965

Top of the world—and going nowhere but up. How many of these questions about the Beatles' heady year of 1965 can you answer? (Answers begin on page 68.)

213 What was the Beatles' first #1 single of 1965 in the United States?

214 During 1963 and 1964, the Beatles were under constant, intense pressure to release new tracks. They proved to be up to the challenge—in America, the group's output was parlayed into six LPs released within a span of twenty-one months!—but they had to appeal to a good many songs written by other artists in order to meet their recording commitments. By the end of 1965, the recording approach had changed, and the group was focusing almost exclusively on its own material. Disregarding the light-hearted rendition of the leering folk number "Maggie Mae" that appears on *Let It Be*, can you name the last two tracks on a UK Beatles album of previously unreleased material to be written by someone other than a member of the band?

A. "Honey Don't" and "Matchbox"
B. "Dizzy Miss Lizzy" and "Act Naturally"
C. "Twist and Shout" and "Chains"

215 Which Beatle made a remark that inspired the title of the album *Rubber Soul*?

216 Other than being composed by Paul McCartney, the songs "Yesterday," "I've Just Seen A Face," and "I'm Down" share an interesting common bond in Beatle history. What is it?

A. They were the last songs recorded before the group embarked on its final world tour.
B. They were all recorded on the same day.
C. They were the first songs to feature secret messages to the Beatles' fans.

217 How many Grammys did the Beatles win in 1965?

A. Three
B. Two
C. Zero

218 Identify the song initially entitled "Scrambled Eggs," whose first working lyric included the phrase, "Oh, my baby, how I love your legs."

219 In 1965, an album track lifted from the British release *Beatles For Sale* was issued as a single in the United States—but not in England—and went all the way to #1. Name it.

220 In 1965, the Beatles recorded a new song that

they considered including on the *Help!* LP, but ended up passing off to P.J. Proby. The song in question ended up on the *Beatles Anthology 2* CD. Name it.

221 In a single three-and-a-half hour session on May 10, 1965, the Beatles completed work on two songs that would fill out the American release *Beatles VI*, a patchwork assemblage consisting primarily of tracks English fans had already heard. They hadn't heard these two, however. Can you name them?

222 John Lennon's follow-up to his successful first book was called *A Spaniard In The Works*. The title wreaks havoc on a British expression, "a spanner in the works." What is the closest American equivalent to this expression?

223 Who nominated the Beatles for their MBEs?

224 True or false: George Harrison was 22 years old at the time he received his MBE from Queen Elizabeth.

1965: HELP!

In color this time! Not quite as inspired as its predecessor, and a little heavier on the four-way-stereotyped-Moptop sauce, the 1965 film *Help!* was still a great ride. It continued the Beatles' remarkable love affair with the moviegoing public. (Remarkable, at least, in that the principals of the film were the first to admit that they possessed precious little in the way of acting skill.) How many of the following questions about *Help!* can you answer?

225 Name the songs the Beatles perform in the film *Help!*

226 In the 1964 film *A Hard Day's Night*, the Beatles are pursued everywhere by screaming, adoring female fans. Not in *Help!*, though. The closest the boys get to a worshipful sea of fans in the latter film: the kindly middle-aged women who wave dutifully as the Fabs enter that strange domicile with four front doors. How many of those doting, waving neighborhood women were there, anyway?

227 Which Beatle sleeps in a bed set beneath the level of the floor of the Beatles' far-too-cool apartment?

228 How did Ringo get the ring that caused the group so much trouble?

229 Name the goddess worshipped by the cultists in *Help!*

   A. Siva
   B. Kaili
   C. Kali

230 At one point in the film, the four lads make a sojourn into an Indian restaurant that gets very menacing, very quickly. What Indian-accented rendition of a Beatles tune plays in the background during this sequence?

   A. "A Hard Day's Night"
   B. "She's A Woman"
   C. "Help!"

231 Identify the actor who utters the following line: "Right, Algernon—my little black bag. I shall be forced to operate."

  A. Victor Spinetti
  B. Peter Sellers
  C. Dudley Moore

232 What role did this actor play in the Beatles' previous film?

233 In the Swiss Alps, a long-distance swimmer appears from beneath the ice after the explosion of the Fiendish Thingie. Where does he want to go?

234 True or false: A topless young woman appears for an extended shot during the film *Help!*

235 True or false: During the film *Help!*, Ringo Starr asks John Lennon, "What was it that first attracted you to me?"

236 Which Beatle takes a bite out of a cymbal during *Help!*?

237 What was the working title of the film *Help!*?

238 True or false: George Harrison first picked up a sitar on the set of the movie *Help!*

239 Name the actor who plays the heavy (?) in *Help!* who would later play Gloucester to Laurence Olivier's King Lear in a memorable 1984 television adaptation of Shakespeare's masterpiece—and Rumpole of the Bailey.

  A. John Gielgud
  B. Leo McKern
  C. John Hurt

240 What is the name of the villain this actor plays in *Help!*?

241 True or false: John Lennon was arrested for possession of marijuana during the filming of *Help!*

242 Where do the Beatles attempt to record "The Night Before" in *Help!*?

243 One of the metal cases with which the underground baddies try to blow up the Beatles while they're playing "The Night Before" bears a curious (and elaborate) inscription. What does the case say?

A. Something about explosives
B. Something about Paul being dead
C. Something about Julian Lennon

244 True or false: During the filming of *Help!*, the Beatles amused themselves by renting four Cadillac limousines and smashing them into things.

245 What taped Beatles song, intended to misdirect the bad guys, is playing underground while the Beatles are playing "The Night Before"?

246 To whom is the film *Help!* dedicated?

━━━━━

247 The British LP release *Help!* (but not the film of the same name) features a track that holds the distinction of being the most-covered tune in the history of popular music. Can you name it—and cite the peculiar irony relating to the song's UK chart history?

248 What was the first released Beatles song to run for more than three minutes?

249 On August 1, 1965, while performing live on the British television show *Blackpool Night Out,* the Beatles did something that, according to George Harrison, they'd never done before. What was it?

250 One of the Beatles #1 hits in the United States from 1965 features, as its title, a Ringoism describing the group's seemingly inhuman work schedule during this period. So, for that matter, does one from 1964. Name them both.

251 The Beatles wanted fourteen tracks for their late-1965 album, but were short by one as recording for *Rubber Soul* drew to a close. Can you name the recording, rejected during the *Help!* sessions, that they polished up at the last minute for inclusion on the new LP?

252 Paul McCartney lapses into a bit of French during the song "Michelle." What does the French part translate to?

253 Ringo Starr plays organ on a track featured on *Rubber Soul.* Identify it.

254 In a move that may or may not have been motivated by a desire to highlight the Beatles' acoustic sound, movers and shakers at Capitol decided to lead off Side One of the American release of the *Rubber Soul* LP with a song that had appeared on the UK version of *Help!* At the same time they removed, among other things, the album's up-tempo British opener, "Drive My

Car." Name the leadoff "folkish" song that helped to alter the overall texture of *Rubber Soul,* making the American version of the album sound much less rock–oriented than the British.

255 Another "folkish" song from the British *Help!* LP showed up on *Rubber Soul.* Name it.

256 True or false: Capitol executives persuaded the Beatles to record an unconvincing cover of Bob Dylan's "Blowin' In The Wind" in the hope of including this track on the American version of *Rubber Soul,* but the Beatles did not think enough of the finished track to issue it.

257 Supply the missing word from George Harrison's *Rubber Soul* track "Think For Yourself": "Although your mind's. . . "

258 The LP *Rubber Soul* features a track with an unprecedented songwriting credit: Lennon/ McCartney/Starkey. Without looking at the back of the sleeve, identify the song.

259 Who plays the elegant keyboard solo on "In My Life"?

A. Billy Preston
B. Nicky Hopkins
C. George Martin

260 What instrument is being played during this segment of "In My Life"?

261 The opening line of John Lennon's disturbing song "Run for Your Life" recalls an old Elvis Presley number, which features the same line. Can you name it?

262 True or false: In 1965, the Beatles dropped in on Elvis Presley in Los Angeles.

263 What Bob Dylan tune is generally regarded as a parody of John Lennon's Dylan-like composition "Norwegian Wood"?

264 You can't get *Beatles '65* on CD—at least, not as of this writing—but you can certainly remember this American record. Or can you? What tracks appeared on this distillation of *Beatles For Sale,* now made obsolete by the release of the authoritative Beatles CD catalog?

265 How many of the tracks appearing on the American-release album *Beatles '65* were released by the Beatles during 1965?

266 Later in 1965, Capitol released yet another "composite" album for the American market, this one entitled *Beatles VI*. How many of the tracks appearing on that disc can you recall?

267 What was the Beatles last #1 single of 1965 in the United States?

Answers

213 "Ticket To Ride"

214 b) Morrison and Russell's "Act Naturally," and Larry Williams' "Dizzy Miss Lizzy," both of which appear on the *Help!* CD. (In the U.S., "Act Naturally" showed up on *Yesterday. . . and Today*; "Dizzy Miss Lizzy" appeared on *Beatles VI*.)

215 Paul McCartney. He was assessing an early

run-through of his own number, "I'm Down," which he dismissed as "plastic soul."

216 b) And the on-the-spot Mr. Versatility Award goes to. . . Paul McCartney. All three numbers were recorded on the very same day! As author Mark Hertsgaard puts it in his book *A Day In The Life,* "June 14, 1965, was a red-letter day for McCartney. . . ." Indeed it was.

217 c) Zero

218 "Yesterday." As dedicated McCartney enthusiasts know, the tune was circulating through Paul McCartney's head one morning immediately after he woke up. He quickly made his way to the piano and established the chord structure, eventually adding in dummy lyrics as well. McCartney was initially suspicious that he had appropriated an old standard of some kind, and had to be convinced, by repeated playings of the tune to friends, that he had in fact developed the tune himself.

219 "Eight Days A Week"

220 "That Means A Lot"

221 "Dizzy Miss Lizzy" and "Bad Boy"

222 "Tossing a monkey wrench into things"

223 Prime Minister Harold Wilson

224 True

225 "Help!," "The Night Before," "You've Got To Hide Your Love Away," "I Need You," "Another Girl," "You're Going To Lose That Girl," and "Ticket To Ride"

226 Two

227 John Lennon

228 A fan sent it to him in a letter.

229 b) Kaili

230 a) "A Hard Day's Night"

231 a) Victor Spinetti

232 The television director

233 The White Cliffs of Dover

234 True. She is receiving a bath from her mother, who is washing off red paint; the young lady's back is, however, decorously turned to the camera.

235 True

236 George Harrison

237 *Eight Arms to Hold You*; Capitol Records issued a version of the "Ticket to Ride" single that described the song as being from that film.

238 True

239 b) Leo "Ah, So" McKern

240 Klang

241 False

242 Salisbury Plain, near Stonehenge

243 a) The case reads, "Equal to exactly one-millionth of all the high explosives exploded in one week of the Second World War."

244 True

245 "She's A Woman"

246 The picture is "respectfully dedicated to the memory of Mr. Elias Howe, who in 1846 invented the sewing machine."

247 The recording is "Yesterday," and the strangest part of its British sixties chart history is that it had none. The Beatles never released the song as a single in their home country during the sixties.

248 "Ticket to Ride"

249 One of them performed solo during a Beatles gig. John Lennon, George Harrison, and Ringo Starr all stepped offstage while Paul McCartney performed "Yesterday."

250 "A Hard Day's Night" and "Eight Days A Week"

251 "Wait"

252 "These are words that go well together."

253 "I'm Looking Through You"

254 "I've Just Seen a Face"

255 "It's Only Love"

256 False

257 The next word is "opaque."

258 "What Goes On"

259 c) Producer George Martin, whose many keyboard contributions to the group's songs may be the chief justification for regarding him as the "Fifth Beatle."

260 An electric piano, although the accelerated speed of the tape makes it sound closer to a harpsichord.

261 "Baby, Let's Play House"

262 True. At one point in the encounter, he is reported to have said, "Look, guys, if you're just going to sit there and stare at me, I'm going to bed."

263 "4th Time Around," which appears on *Blonde On Blonde*.

264 Side One: "No Reply," "I'm A Loser," "Baby's In Black," "Rock And Roll Music," "I'll Follow The Sun," "Mr. Moonlight." Side Two: "Honey Don't," "I'll Be Back," "She's A Woman," "I Feel Fine," "Everybody's Trying To Be My Baby."

265 None of them.

266 Side One: "Kansas City/Hey-Hey-Hey-Hey!," "Eight Days A Week," "You Like Me Too Much," "Bad Boy," "I Don't Want To Spoil The Party," "Words Of Love." Side Two: "What You're Doing," "Yes It Is," "Dizzy Miss Lizzy," "Tell Me What You See," "Every Little Thing."

267 "We Can Work It Out"

ten

TITLE TALK

How familiar are you with the names of the various Beatles songs? You're about to find out! Note: The following questions take as their "universe" of song titles all the Beatles' single releases, plus the complete British releases *Please Please Me, With the Beatles, A Hard Day's Night, Help!, Rubber Soul, Revolver, Sgt. Pepper's Lonely Hearts Club Band, Magical Mystery Tour, The Beatles, Yellow Submarine, Abbey Road,* and *Let It Be.* (Answers appear on page 74.)

268 What Beatles song boasts the longest title?

269 Three Beatles songs feature exclamation points in their (correctly rendered) titles. Can you name them?

270 Counting parenthetical statements as part of a song title, there are nineteen Beatles songs that use a single word as a title. How many can you name? (Words to the wise: "Anna (Go To Him)" and "Money (That's What I Want)" don't count, as their official, published titles extend beyond a single word.)

271 There are three Beatles songs whose titles are phrased in the form of a question. Can you name them?

272 There is only one Beatles song whose title begins with the letter *J.* What is it?

273 Name the four Beatles songs that feature the word "bird" as part of the title.

Answers

268 "Everybody's Got Something To Hide Except Me And My Monkey."

269 "Help!," "Oh! Darling," and "Being For The Benefit Of Mr Kite!"

270 The nineteen songs: "Because," "Birthday," "Blackbird," "Boys," "Chains," "Flying," "Girl," "Help!," "Julia," "Matchbox," "Michelle," "Misery," "Piggies," "Rain," "Revolution," "Something," "Taxman," "Wait," and "Yesterday."

271 "Do You Want To Know a Secret?," "What Goes On?," and "Why Don't We Do It In the Road?"

272 "Julia"

273 "And Your Bird Can Sing," "Blackbird," "Free As A Bird," and "Norwegian Wood (This Bird Has Flown)." By the way, "Free As A Bird" counts, because it was released as a Beatles single in 1995!

eleven
1966

Things started getting weird in '66—sometimes in ways the Beatles weren't so crazy about (road hassles, media volcanoes), and sometimes in ways they took a shining to for a while (surrealism and the occasional hallucinatory journey). How many of these questions about 1966 can you answer? (See page 81 for answers.)

274 True or false: Donovan was secretly asked to join the Beatles in early 1966, but he declined.

275 In 1966, following standard four-American-Beatles-albums-for-every-three-English-releases procedure, Capitol Records took stock of its material. It found a track or two skimmed from the British LP *Help!*, a few lifted from the British LP *Rubber Soul,* both sides of a previously released single, and a few tracks from the forthcoming *Revolver.* Capitol then banded all the tracks together and started pressing its newest megahit album. Can you name the collage-like American LP that ended up making many U.S. Beatles fans conclude (erroneously) that John Lennon must have been on vacation for the bulk of the *Revolver* sessions?

276 What was controversial about this patchwork album's original cover?

277 The album *Revolver*, released in 1966, was the first of the Beatles' albums to be significantly affected by the hallucinogenic drug LSD. Which Beatles were the first to take LSD? Under what circumstances did they do so?

278 Who was the last Beatle to take LSD?

279 True or false: A working title of George Harrison's "I Want To Tell You" was "I Don't Know," inspired by George Harrison's response to a question about what he intended to call the song.

280 What was the working title of John Lennon's first real foray into psychedelic music, "Tomorrow Never Knows"?

281 Which Beatle came up with the odd title for the song "Tomorrow Never Knows"?

282 What sacred book inspired John Lennon's "Tomorrow Never Knows"?

283 True or false: John Lennon originally wanted the track "Tomorrow Never Knows" to feature chanting Tibetan monks.

284 How was John Lennon's lead vocal track altered on this song?

   A. A jack was inserted in Lennon's neck.

B. The vocal track was fed through an organ speaker.

C. Lennon screamed at a microphone that was wired into the hollow part of an empty peanut butter jar.

285 With whom was John Lennon talking when he had the experience that formed the basis of the song "She Said She Said"?

A. Jane Fonda
B. Peter Fonda
C. Henry Fonda

286 Two of John Lennon's songs on the UK version of *Revolver* feature the image of floating on a stream in their lyrics. Name them.

287 What was the produce-inspired working title of "I Want to Tell You?"

288 Who plays the memorable guitar solo in "Taxman"?

289 True or false: John Lennon composed and recorded a song protesting American involvement in Vietnam that nearly made it onto the album *Revolver*, but met with a Brian Epstein veto.

290 Who was Eleanor Rigby?

291 How was the name "McKenzie" selected for inclusion in the song "Eleanor Rigby"?

292 What was Father McKenzie's (overly familiar) last name in the song's earlier incarnation?

293 Two songs on *Revolver* feature titles that do not

appear at any point in the lyrics of the songs in question. Can you name them?

294 *Revolver* featured three, count 'em, three songs composed by George Harrison. Before the Beatles broke up in 1970, one of their official releases would boast *four* Harrisongs. Name it—and, for extra credit, name all four of the songs.

295 Alternate take department: Upon the release of *The Beatles Anthology 2,* fans were able to hear an intriguing 1966 version of George Harrison's "Taxman" in which the phrase "Ah-ah, Mr. Wilson, ah-ah, Mr. Heath" had been replaced by something else. What showed up in place of this familiar part of the song?

296 To whom do the familiar gibes at Mr. Wilson and Mr. Heath in this song refer? (British fans, please excuse yourselves from the discussion and talk amongst yourselves for a moment.)

297 True or false: The 95 percent tax rate of which George Harrison complains in "Taxman" was a literal fact, not a piece of poetic exaggeration.

298 The album *Revolver* featured a first—a Beatles track on which no member of the band made any instrumental contribution whatsoever. Can you name it?

299 True or false: Longtime Beatles insider Klaus Voormann appears on the cover of the album *Revolver.*

300 True or false: A dot-and-dash message spelling the word "pot" in Morse code appears on the cover of the *Revolver* album.

301 What country banned public broadcast of all Beatles music as a result of John Lennon's remarks about the relative popularity of his band and Jesus Christ?

302 How long did this ban last?

303 True or false: At the time of John Lennon's public apology for supposedly blasphemous remarks, the Beatles had the #1 single in the United States.

304 The Beatles were awarded a Grammy in 1966 for Song Of The Year for a recording they had not issued as a single in the United States. Identify it.

  A. "Michelle"
  B. "Tomorrow Never Knows"
  C. "Taxman"

305 Paul McCartney won a 1966 Grammy in the category Best Contemporary Pop Vocal Performance, Male. For what song was he given this award?

  A. "Good Day Sunshine"
  B. "Eleanor Rigby"
  C. "For No One"

306 True or false: Paul McCartney was involved in a serious automobile accident in November, 1966.

1966: CRYPTIC LYRIC ALERT

Along about 1966, the Beatles' lyrics started to get a little. . . odd. Identify the Beatles songs from this year that feature:

307 The singer's insistence that there's no time to attach a sign to him.

308 A woman (?) who's seen seven wonders and possesses a green bird.

309 A face kept in a jar.

310 The singer's instruction to turn off one's mind.

311 Corpses instructed on the finer points of tax strategy.

════════

312 On November 9, 1966, John Lennon was in attendance at a preview of an art show entitled *Unfinished Paintings and Objects*. What notable individual did he meet for the first time at this event?

313 True or false: Shortly after the conclusion of the Beatles' 1966 U.S. tour, George Harrison left for India to study music.

314 In the backing vocals for "Paperback Writer," the Beatles chant a nursery rhyme. Identify it.

315 It was late 1966, and the Beatles had neglected to complete an LP in time for the Christmas shopping season! What compilation consisting primarily of Beatles singles did Parlophone assemble for a December release in Britain?

A. *A Collection Of Beatles Oldies*

B. *Accountants' Maneuver*

C. *Mistletoe Music*

316 What was the Beatles' only #1 single of 1966 in the United States?

Answers

274 False. No such offer was ever extended.

275 *Yesterday. . . and Today*

276 It featured the Beatles holding dismembered baby dolls and raw meat. The cover photograph caused a scandal and was quickly replaced with a less graphic shot of the lovable lads posed near a trunk. The replacement may well have been the more subversive of the two shots, however: the Beatles posed around the trunk look distinctly stoned.

277 John and George. A dentist they both knew put some into their coffee without their knowledge.

278 Paul McCartney

279 True. Harrison seems to have had a good deal of difficulty coming up with song titles during this period. Given the bizarre working title of "I Want To Tell You," it's easy to hypothesize that the baffling name of the other *Revolver* Harrisong, "Love You To," could have been the result of a similar on-the-spot improvisation along the following lines: Someone-Other-Than George Harrison, "So—do you want *me* to name the song for you?" George Harrison, "Love you to." This, however, is pure speculation!

280 "Mark I" (So say the recording sheets and tape

box labels of the session. "Mark I" is apparently a British rough equivalent of "Version I.")

281 Ringo Starr. The phrase means, roughly, "Who knows what tomorrow may bring." In the televised documentary *The Beatles Anthology,* John Lennon, via an earlier interview, explained that he chose what he thought to be a humorous title for the song because he was worried about the composition being perceived as pretentious. In fact, the vague title only added to the sense of mystery around this unusual recording. For a superb essay on the song and the emerging drug culture it mirrored, see Ian MacDonald's extraordinary book *Revolution in the Head,* the strongest and most intellectually rigorous piece of work on the Beatles that any of us is likely to encounter.

282 *The Tibetan Book of the Dead,* as discussed in Timothy Leary's *The Psychedelic Experience.*

283 True

284 b) It was routed through the rotating speaker of an organ.

285 b) Actor Peter Fonda. Fonda was trying to describe the details of what he claimed was a near-death experience; Lennon, under the influence of hallucinogens, was in no mood to discuss the matter.

286 "I'm Only Sleeping," which appeared on *Yesterday. . . and Today* in the U.S., and "Tomorrow Never Knows."

287 "Laxton's Superb." Harrison was in the habit of

assigning the names of apples to his unnamed tracks during this period.

288 Paul McCartney

289 False

290 She was a Liverpudlian woman from the first half of the century whose gravestone predates the composition of the Beatles' melancholy song. A woman of the Rigby family with the first name Eleanor is buried in St. Peter's churchyard in Woolton, near Paul McCartney's former suburban Allerton home. Her tombstone—or a digitized approximation of it—appears prominently in the 1995 *Free As A Bird* video. Eleanor died in 1939. There are, however, other facts to bear in mind here: Paul McCartney's fascination with the name "Eleanor" is apparently linked with his having worked with the actress Eleanor Bron in the movie *Help!*, and his use of the name "Rigby" has been connected to a shop window display he saw. That said, it seems hard to deny that the Rigby gravestone could have served as an influence, subconscious or otherwise, for the striking song about death that he wrote for the *Revolver* LP.

291 By paging through phone book listings

292 McCartney

293 "Love You To" and "Tomorrow Never Knows"

294 The release: the double album *The Beatles* (a.k.a. *The White Album*). The songs: "While My Guitar Gently Weeps," "Piggies," "Long Long Long," and "Savoy Truffle."

295 A high-speed backing vocal in which the phrase "Anybody got a bit of money?" is repeated.

296 Harold Wilson was England's prime minister and head of the Labour government; Edward Heath was the leader of the Conservative party, and later prime minister.

297 True. Actually, the top tax rate at the time was an astonishing 96 percent, according to Apple insider Peter Brown, who writes about the subject in his book *The Love You Make*. Such tax figures inspired genuine—and understand-able—concern to Harrison, who had appar-ently just come to understand exactly how much of the group's earnings the government was claiming.

298 "Eleanor Rigby"

299 True. Voormann, who created the cover, incor-porated a photograph of himself immediately below his own signature. Look right under the mouth of the large drawing of John.

300 False

301 South Africa

302 Five years

303 False. "Yellow Submarine" only reached #2 in America.

304 a) "Michelle"

305 b) "Eleanor Rigby"

306 False. This mythical accident was said to be the cause of McCartney's early "demise," and of the many "clues" supposedly inserted in Beatle songs and sleeve covers following the event. But see question #379 for a real-life incident during the same time period that may have helped to inspire the various fantasies.

307 "Love You To"

308 "And Your Bird Can Sing"

309 "Eleanor Rigby"

310 "Tomorrow Never Knows"

311 "Taxman"

312 Yoko Ono

313 True

314 "Frere Jacques"

315 a) *A Collection Of Beatles Oldies*

316 "Paperback Writer." The band's follow-up, "Yellow Submarine," only reached #2, leaving "Paperback Writer" as its only American #1 of the year.

twelve
COVERS, ETCETERA

How well do you know the covers and sleeves of the various Beatles albums? Check the questions below and find out. (Answers begin on page 88.)

317 True or false: On the cover of the British *Help!* album, the four Beatles are pictured spelling out the word "help" in semaphore.

318 The twin greatest-hits compilations known informally as The Blue Album and The Red Album feature startling cover shots: early-sixties and late-sixties Beatles in exactly the same pose, looking down at the camera from an apartment stairwell. For what original purpose was each photograph taken?

319 Name, in order, the Beatles who are walking across the street on the cover of *Abbey Road*.

320 What color is the Volkswagen visible behind George Harrison on the cover of *Abbey Road*?

321 Which Beatle has thrust his hands into his pockets on the cover of *Abbey Road*?

322 Which Beatle is barefoot on the cover of *Abbey Road*?

323 What was the first Beatles LP to feature a cover on which the word "Beatles" is nowhere to be found?

324 Name the artist who designed the *Sgt. Pepper's Lonely Hearts Club Band* cover.

325 Which Beatle wears a bright blue uniform on the cover of *Sgt. Pepper's Lonely Hearts Club Band*?

326 Which Beatle wears a green uniform on the cover of *Sgt. Pepper's Lonely Hearts Club Band?*

327 Which Beatle wears a shocking pink uniform on the cover of *Sgt. Pepper's Lonely Hearts Club Band*?

328 Which Beatle wears an orange uniform on the cover of *Sgt. Pepper's Lonely Hearts Club Band?*

329 Identify the British Beatles album that features these words in its liner notes: "It isn't a pot-boiling quick-sale any-old-thing-will-do-for-Christmas mixture."

330 Identify the Beatles album with liner notes that claimed, "(The group's) own built-in tune-smith team of John Lennon and Paul McCartney has already tucked away enough self-penned numbers to maintain a steady out-put of all-original singles from now until 1975!"

331 Which Beatles LP features sleeve notes that promise, "This is a new phase Beatles album"?

Answers

317 False. The "word" is, we are told, NUJV. Perhaps there's some mystical significance. . . and perhaps not.

318 The earlier shot was the cover photograph for the band's first LP, *Please Please Me;* the later shot was meant to grace the cover of the back-to-basics, guaranteed-not-an-overdub-within-a-mile project that began life as *Get Back,* but soon got very complicated indeed and was transformed into *Let It Be.* A different cover idea was eventually employed for *Let It Be.*

319 George Harrison, Paul McCartney, Ringo Starr, and John Lennon

320 White

321 John Lennon

322 Paul McCartney

323 *Rubber Soul*

324 Peter Blake

325 Paul McCartney

326 John Lennon

327 Ringo Starr

328 George Harrison

329 *Beatles For Sale*, which, although certainly superior to any number of pop albums of the era, does in fact display a certain hastily assembled "Christmas rush" feeling.

330 *Please Please Me.* The claim was a ludicrous exaggeration.

331 *Let It Be.* If the "phase" was indeed new—a dubious claim, considering the pre-*Abbey Road* vintage of most of the tracks on the album—it was certainly brief!

thirteen
Looks Like Rain. . .

Lots of Beatles songs incorporate rain imagery. How many of the following songs that do can you identify? (Answers begin on 91.)

332 A Beatles song about home repair? Sure, if the roof's leaking. Identify the tune.

333 A rough night—but the rain washes it away. What Beatles song includes this image?

334 On this 1966 B side, John Lennon goes Buddhist for a bit, using a crowd's reaction to a rainstorm as a metaphor for the human tendency to affix "good" and "bad" labels to any situation. Provide the title of this song, and identify the technical innovation it incorporates.

335 In what Beatles song does a banker neglect to wear a coat during a rainstorm?

336 In what Beatles song does the singer opine that standing in an English rainstorm can lead to a suntan?

337 Name the 1964-release song in which someone complains that his tears are falling like rain.

338 Name the song that discusses the relative futility of saving up one's money for a rainy day.

339 In what song does John Lennon sing about words that drop, one by one, like rain into a cup?

340 Name the Beatles song in which Paul McCartney decides to pursue the sunshine because there may be rain tomorrow.

341 What song uses rain imagery and features a first line that makes reference to a sheepdog?

342 Name the song in which someone sings of wearing a raincoat and standing in the sun.

343 One of the Beatles' very earliest hits features a line about rain always being in the singer's heart. Which song is it?

344 There is a Beatles song in which the lead vocalist fantasizes about escaping a storm by heading undersea. Identify the song and the singer.

Answers

332 "Fixing A Hole"

333 "The Long And Winding Road"

334 "Rain." It features the first use of a backwards vocal track on a Beatles recording.

335 "Penny Lane"

336 "I Am The Walrus"

337 "I'm A Loser"

338 "The Ballad Of John And Yoko"

339 "Across The Universe"

340 "I'll Follow The Sun"

341 "Hey Bulldog." You were thinking, perhaps of "Martha, My Dear," which immortalized Paul McCartney's pooch? Sorry.

342 "Two Of Us"

343 "Please Please Me"

344 "Octopus's Garden"—the lead vocalist is, of course, Ringo Starr.

fourteen

1967

I t was. . . beautiful, man. Just beautiful. Try your
hand at these questions from the trippy year of
1967, but remember: If you get too many right, you
weren't really there the first time around. (Answers
begin on page 107.)

345 What real-life place inspired John Lennon to
write "Strawberry Fields Forever"?

   A. A reform school called "Strawberry Field"
   B. A lunatic asylum called "Strawberry Field"
   C. A bus stop called "Strawberry Field"

346 The 1967 release "Penny Lane"/"Strawberry
Fields Forever" failed to reach the #1 spot in
the UK; the record climbed only as high as the
second position there. What group or artist
kept the Beatles out of the top slot?

   A. The Mamas and the Papas
   B. Engelbert Humperdinck
   C. The Rolling Stones

347 What instrument is used to play the introductory notes of "Strawberry Fields Forever," as it appears on the CD *Magical Mystery Tour*?

A. A mellotron
B. A harmonium
C. A harmonica

348 Which Beatle plays this introduction?

1967: CRYPTIC LYRIC ALERT

Which 1967 Beatles songs feature the following unusual references in their lyrics?

349 A barber who shows off photos of all his past customers.

350 An unorthodox ascent of the Eiffel Tower.

351 A fireman who carries an hourglass and continually polishes his fire engine.

352 A young lady's encounter with a gentleman from the "motor trade."

353 The singer's brusque dismissal of a dying man's chance of pulling through.

354 A Penguin chanting the "Hare Krishna."

355 The singer's uncertain declaration of himself as the solitary resident of a tree.

356 The storing of cash at the local zoo.

357 An attack upon Edgar Allan Poe.

358 True or false: In 1967, the Beatles paid for a full-page advertisement in *The Times* for the legalization of marijuana.

359 One track that appears on the *Sgt. Pepper's Lonely Hearts Club* album is an early composition the Beatles would appeal to when their amplifiers broke down during club appearances. Name it.

    A. "When I'm Sixty-Four"
    B. "Good Morning Good Morning"
    C. "A Day In The Life"

360 True or false: In the original opening lines of "With A Little Help From My Friends," John Lennon and Paul McCartney had Billy Shears asking his audience whether they would throw tomatoes at him if he went off-key.

361 Is the sound at the end of "Within You Without You" that of a group of people laughing—or crying?

362 True or false: *Sgt. Pepper's Lonely Hearts Club Band* won a Grammy as Album of the Year in 1967.

363 Can you identify the instruments played by the Beatles during the recording of "She's Leaving Home"?

364 During the song "Good Morning Good Morning," John Lennon informs his listeners that the time has come for a spot of tea—and for "Meet The Wife." "What was Meet The Wife"?

    A. A radio program
    B. A television program
    C. A magazine

365 Two songs intended for release on the album that would become *Sgt. Pepper's Lonely Hearts Club Band* were instead issued as the two sides of a new single. Name the two songs that narrowly missed making *Pepper*'s running list as a result of this choice.

366 In post-breakup interviews, John Lennon expressed skepticism about the "concept" underlying the *Sgt. Pepper* album, arguing that the only real unifying theme on the record, beyond the open-ended idea of a fictitious band, was the reprise of the introductory song near the end of the album. There was originally to have been a more substantial concept to the LP, but it was never carried through by the Beatles. What was it?

367 During recording sessions for one of the songs on *Sgt. Pepper's Lonely Hearts Club Band*, George Martin instructed the session musicians as follows: ". . . whatever you do, don't listen to the fellow next to you because I don't want you to be doing the same thing." What song was being recorded?

368 How many grandchildren are evoked during "When I'm Sixty-Four"? What are their names?

369 A television advertisement served as the inspiration for "Good Morning Good Morning." What product was being hawked?

370 True or false: In 1967, the Beatles broadcast a special television documentary based on film shot during the making of *Sgt. Pepper's Lonely Hearts Club Band*.

371 True or false: Unaware that John Lennon was tripping on acid, producer George Martin took the queasy Beatle to the studio roof to take in some fresh air. . . and was shortly met by a panicked George Harrison and Paul McCartney, who had dashed up to reclaim their partner before he flung himself from the top of the railing-free building.

372 True or false: Conservative American commentator William F. Buckley, Jr., visiting London at the time, was invited to attend the orchestral sessions of "A Day In The Life."

1967: GOING TO THE SOURCE WITH MR. LENNON

John Lennon's song "Being For The Benefit Of Mr. Kite!" was inspired by an 1843 circus poster. Can you guess which of the following elements appeared only in the song, and not on the poster?

373 The hogshead of real fire.

374 Mr. H's challenge to the world.

375 The assurance that the act in question has been some days in preparation.

376 The waltzing horse.

377 The promise that Mr. H's somersets will be performed on solid ground.

---

378 What was John Lennon's inspiration for the song "Lucy In The Sky With Diamonds"?

379 What news story in the January 17, 1967, *Daily Mail* inspired John Lennon to write, in "A Day In The Life," about the young man who failed to notice that the lights had changed?

380 A news story about an alarming number of holes in Blackburn, Lancashire, appeared on the very next page of that day's *Daily Mail,* and prompted John Lennon to write what became the third verse of "A Day In The Life." In the Beatles' song, the holes were surrealistically transposed to the confines of the Albert Hall, but where did the holes reside while they were still (supposedly) a hard news story?

381 What film is alluded to in the second verse of "A Day In The Life," the one in which the English army wins the war?

382 What role did John Lennon play in this film?

    A. Private Gripweed
    B. Ensign Pulver
    C. Mister Roberts

383 Identify the Beatles song whose introduction was inspired by the menacing up-and-down wail of an English police car driving near John Lennon's home.

384 What Beatles insider can be heard counting in the background during "A Day In The Life?"

    A. Mal Evans
    B. Peter Brown
    C. Neil Aspinall

385 What track on the *Sgt. Pepper's Lonely Hearts Club Band* album seems to contain a startling—

and apparently heartfelt—*mea culpa* from John Lennon on the subject of wifebeating?

   A. "Getting Better"
   B. "Within You Without You"
   C. "A Day In The Life"

386 True or false: George Harrison plays sitar on the song "Within You Without You."

387 During a preliminary take of one of the songs on the *Sgt. Pepper's Lonely Hearts Club Band* album, John Lennon's count-in consisted of the words "sugarplum fairy, sugarplum fairy." Identify the song.

388 True or false: The final sequencing of the tracks for *Sgt. Pepper's Lonely Hearts Club Band* was determined by consulting the Chinese oracle the *I Ching.*

389 Name the legendary performer who opened his act with a rendition of "Sgt. Pepper's Lonely Hearts Club Band" only two days after the album had been released.

   A. James Brown
   B. Ronnie Hawkins
   C. Jimi Hendrix

1967: THE <u>SGT. PEPPER</u> COVER

Pull out your copy of *Sgt. Pepper's Lonely Hearts Club Band* and take a good look at the cover. Identify:

390 The third face down from the top on the left-hand side of the album.

391 The man immediately to the left of the bespectacled John Lennon.

392 The male at the uppermost right corner of the assembly.

393 The woman posing languidly, directly to the right of the psychedelically clad George Harrison.

394 The man who looks as though he's ready to travel, and whose face is situated directly above the waxwork Ringo Starr's head.

395 The boxer on the far left side of the front row.

396 The startled-looking gent in the back row, fourth from the left.

397 The man situated directly in front of the startled-looking gent's tie.

398 The man wearing Arab headgear on the far right.

399 The man immediately to the right of Marilyn Monroe, who is located near the center of the second row from the top.

400 The man immediately to the right of W.C. Fields in the top row.

401 The young girl situated immediately above the small television set near the letter *S* in the word "Beatles."

402 The bearded fellow to the right of the cartoon image of Oliver Hardy, in the second row from the top.

403 The mustachioed gentleman immediately to the bearded fellow's right.

404 The gentleman with no shirt on situated directly behind Ringo, who is decked out in a psychedelic band uniform.

405 The bearded man immediately above George's hat.

406 The tough-looking dame in the top row, third from the left.

407 The man immediately beneath the tough-looking dame.

408 The unlikely pair of Americans in the middle of the top row.

409 The competing band mentioned by name on the cover of the album.

410 The Beatles had planned to include two particularly memorable faces in the *Sgt. Pepper* cover shot, but they reconsidered. One of the people in question is frequently cited as the most evil figure of the twentieth century; the other is frequently cited as the most revered. Name them both.

411 Now for the bonus question: Other than the Beatles themselves, there's only one person who appears *twice* on the cover of *Sgt. Pepper's Lonely Hearts Club Band* cover. Who is it?

═══════════

412 How much time elapsed between the last studio work on *Sgt. Pepper's Lonely Hearts Club*

Band and the first sessions for their next recording project?

A. Six months
B. Three weeks
C. Four days

413 Complete the sentence: "Away in the sky, beyond the clouds, live 4 or 5 magicians. By casting Wonderful Spells they turn the Most Ordinary Coach Trip into a. . . "

414 Name the Beatle wife who missed the train bound for Bangor, Wales, where the Beatles would spend a weekend with Maharishi Mahesh Yogi.

415 Who brought Maharishi Mahesh Yogi to the attention of the Beatles?

A. Patti Harrison
B. Donovan
C. Jane Asher

416 What fateful event took place while the Beatles were studying Transcendental Meditation during their trip to Wales?

417 What was the first new song the Beatles began recording in the aftermath of this unexpected event?

A. "It's All Too Much"
B. "I Am The Walrus"
C. "Baby You're A Rich Man"

418 How many times does George Harrison repeat the phrase "don't be long" in "Blue Jay Way"?

A. Eleven
B. Twenty-nine
C. Sixty-one

419 Of the following people, only one was *not* in attendance as the Beatles laid down tracks for their single "All You Need Is Love" before a worldwide television audience. Can you spot the person who doesn't belong in the following list? Eric Clapton, Marianne Faithfull, Mick Jagger, Michael McCartney, Keith Moon, Graham Nash, Keith Richards, James Taylor.

420 True or false: Immediately after the taping of "All You Need Is Love," a protracted fistfight broke out involving several of the pop VIPs in the studio.

421 Identify the musical compositions by other artists quoted at various points of "All You Need Is Love."

422 True or false: John Lennon can be heard chewing gum during the song "All You Need Is Love."

423 At the end of "All You Need Is Love," someone starts singing a repeated line from an old Beatles hit. What is it?

A. "Please Please Me"
B. "She Loves You"
C. "From Me To You"

424 True or false: The endearingly disgusting lyric about yellow stuff dripping from the eye of a dead dog that appears in "I Am The Walrus" has its origin in a Liverpool schoolyard chant.

425 What is the subtitle listed for "I Am The Walrus" on the album *Magical Mystery Tour*?

    A. "Or, What You Will"
    B. "'No You're Not,' Said Little Nicola"
    C. "Cliff's Notes Available At A Reasonable Price"

426 One of the Beatles' best-known songs of 1967 incorporates a lead guitar solo from George Harrison that collapses midway through. What song is it?

    A. "All You Need Is Love"
    B. "Baby You're A Rich Man"
    C. "Penny Lane"

427 Pull out your copy of *Magical Mystery Tour* and take a look at the album cover. All four Beatles appear masked. Can you guess which Beatle is which?

428 The eleven-song collection known as *Magical Mystery Tour* has emerged as one of the Beatles' most popular "albums"—and is even cited by John Lennon as "one of my favorite[s]. . . 'cos it's so weird" during the televised documentary *The Beatles Anthology*. Yet the various tracks in question were never conceived as parts of an LP. Name the songs from the film that appeared on the British double-45 package that formed the core of the later album release.

429 What type of food does John Lennon supply in his memorable role as a waiter in the film *Magical Mystery Tour*?

430 Which Beatle sports a strange white cap dur-

ing the "I Am The Walrus" sequence of the
film *Magical Mystery Tour*?

1967: FORCES TO BE RECKONED WITH

No longer simply teen idols, the Beatles emerged
in 1967 as cultural figures of note. Identify the
sources of the following remarks, all of them made
by self-appointed experts or Established Institutions
who weighed in with opinions about the Fabs during the heady year of 1967 or shortly thereafter.
Actually, not quite *all* of the following remarks are
on the level. One of the quotes that follows is
bogus. Can you spot it?

431 "[Some of the more recent Beatles songs] show
an acute awareness of the principles of rhythm
and brainwashing. Neither Lennon nor
McCartney were world-beaters in school. For
them to have written some of their songs is like
someone who had not had physics or math
inventing the A-bomb. . . . Because of its technical excellence, it is possible that this music is
put together by behavioral scientists. . . . "

432 "Mr. Lennon's messianic pretensions are a matter of record, and are well known to the world
at large and to the members of this
Government. . . . [Although] the suitability of
his group's recent recordings for public broadcast are, thankfully, no concern of this office, an
honest assessment of the most recent release
from this group compels the observation that
its authors are given to drug use. I shall, I think,
surprise no one when I note that these individ-
uals are more in the habit of encouraging oth-

ers to follow their example on this score than is likely to suit the taste of this Prime Minister."

433 "[The release of the album *Sgt. Pepper's Lonely Hearts Club Band* is] a decisive moment in the history of Western civilisation."

434 "I declare that John Lennon, George Harrison, Paul McCartney, and Ringo Starr are mutants, prototypes of a new race of laughing freemen."

435 "Oh, I get it. You don't want to be cute anymore."

436 "[Paul McCartney is] an irresponsible idiot."

437 "The Beatles exemplify. . . a new and golden renaissance of song."

———

438 What immortal song do the Beatles, under the collective pseudonym "The Ravellers," perform on their 1967 Christmas fan-club disc?

    A. "Pull Me Closer, Harold"
    B. "Plenty Of Jam Jars"
    C. "'Twas The Night Before Christmas"

439 On the 1967 Christmas disc, the Beatles sing the praises of an imaginary product that is intended for use on one's trousers and one's hair. What is it called?

    A. Apple Zapple
    B. Romeo Gold
    C. Wonderlust

440 What was the Beatles' last #1 single of 1967 in the United States?

Answers

345 a) A reform school for girls in Liverpool

346 b) Engelbert Humperdinck, with "Release Me"

347 a) A mellotron, an early forerunner of the synthesizer

348 Paul McCartney

349 "Penny Lane"

350 "I Am The Walrus"

351 "Penny Lane"

352 "She's Leaving Home"

353 "Good Morning Good Morning." The sinister overtones of this song's first few lines are often overlooked.

354 "I Am The Walrus"

355 "Strawberry Fields Forever"

356 "Baby You're A Rich Man"

357 "I Am The Walrus"

358 True

359 a) "When I'm Sixty-Four." Apparently Paul McCartney resuscitated the number after his father's sixty-fourth birthday jogged his memory of the tune.

360 True. Ringo Starr, mindful of the group's experience of being pelted with handfuls of a type of candy they'd mentioned liking, refused to sing the line. The song's opening was rewritten, thus avoiding tense encounters with produce-bearing Beatles people.

361 Laughing, according to the world's preeminent Beatleologist Ian MacDonald.

362 True. It also won for Best Album Cover, Best Contemporary Rock 'n' Roll Recording, and Best Engineered Recording.

363 There are none. A group of string musicians handled all the playing.

364 b) A television situation comedy, popular in Britain at the time, starring Thora Hird and Freddie Frinton.

365 "Strawberry Fields Forever" and "Penny Lane." The move arose due to Brian Epstein's concern that the Beatles, who had not released any new material since the summer of the previous year, had been too long absent from the UK pop charts.

366 The original idea was to record an album of songs that related to the Beatles' childhood memories of Liverpool; the first two tracks laid down with this intent were "Strawberry Fields Forever" and "Penny Lane," appropriated for a sublime pre-*Pepper* single.

367 "A Day In The Life." The recipients of Martin's unusual advice were some rather perplexed classical musicians, who were there to supply the two rising symphonic tornadoes that appear in that song.

368 Three: Vera, Chuck, and Dave.

369 Kellogg's Corn Flakes.

370 False. The special was discussed, but never broadcast. The 1995 televised documentary *The Beatles Anthology* featured some decidedly trippy footage—intended for the planned 1967 special—shot during recording sessions for "A Day In The Life."

371 True. It should be noted that Lennon apparently took the LSD by mistake on this occasion; most sources indicate that the group did not try to work while hallucinating on acid!

372 False. One senses it would have been a uniquely spirited encounter, though.

373 See below

374 See below

375 See below

376 See below

377 Of the elements cited, only the waltzing horse is an original Lennon contribution. John's deft reworking of the material before him, however, provides one of the rare instances in which fans can observe his extraordinary creative process as it unfolds on a line-by-line basis. Pull out the lyric sheet for *Sgt. Pepper's Lonely Hearts Club Band* and compare the words to "Being For The Benefit Of Mr. Kite!" to the following text of the 1843 poster, available via the Internet: "Pablo Fanque's Circus Royal, Town-Meadows, Rochdale. Grandest Night of the Season! And positively the last night but three! Being for the benefit of Mr Kite late of Wells's circus and Mr

J. Henderson, the celebrated somerset thrower! Wire dancer, vaulter, rider, etc. On Tuesday evening, February 14th, 1843, Messrs. Kite & Henderson, in announcing the following Entertainment, assure the Public that this Night's Production will be one of the most Splendid ever produced in this Town, having been some days in preparation. Mr Kite will, for this Night only, introduce the celebrated horse, Zanthus! Well known to be one of the best Broke Horses in the world!!! Mr Henderson will undertake the arduous Task of throwing twenty-one somersets on the solid ground. Mr Kite will appear, for the first time this season, On the Tight Rope, When Two Gentleman Amateurs of this Town will perform with him. Mr Henderson will, for the first time in Rochdale, introduce his extraordinary Trampoline Leaps and Somersets! Over Men & Horses, through Hoops, over Garters, and lastly, through a Hogshead of Real Fire! In this branch of the profession, Mr H challenges The World!"

378 His son Julian's painting of a school companion.

379 A story relating to the death of Guinness heir Tara Browne, a friend of the Beatles (and, indeed, of many in their circle). He had been riding with Paul McCartney when McCartney was involved in a minor moped accident in November of the previous year; in the later accident that killed him, he had run a red light and collided with a van. Some of Browne's friends—notably John Lennon—assumed that Browne had been under the influence of LSD at the time of his death.

380 In the road. The story read as follows: "There are 4,000 holes in the road in Blackburn, Lancashire, or one twenty-sixth of a hole per person, according to a council survey. If Blackburn is typical there are two million holes in Britain's roads and 300,000 in London."

381 The film in question is *How I Won The War.*

382 a) Private Gripweed

383 "I Am The Walrus"

384 a) Mal Evans

385 a) "Getting Better." In an interview with *Playboy* magazine, Lennon later admitted that the lyric was autobiographical.

386 True

387 "A Day In The Life." A version of the song incorporating the "sugarplum fairy" opening appears on the double-disc set *The Beatles Anthology 2.*

388 False

389 c) Jimi Hendrix

390 Stuart Sutcliffe, the Beatles' first bassist

391 Oscar Wilde

392 Bob Dylan

393 Marlene Dietrich

394 Marlon Brando

395 Sonny Liston

396 Lenny Bruce

397 Dylan Thomas

398 T.E. Lawrence

399 William Burroughs

400 Carl Jung

401 Shirley Temple

402 Karl Marx

403 H.G. Wells

404 Johnny Weismuller, of "Tarzan" movie fame

405 George Bernard Shaw—or, at any rate, a photograph of a wax figure of him

406 Mae West

407 Aldous Huxley

408 Edgar Allan Poe and Fred Astaire

409 The Rolling Stones

410 Adolf Hitler and Mahatma Gandhi

411 Shirley Temple, who shows up, as we have seen, above the television situated near the letter *S* in the word "Beatles." She is also the figure on the far rightmost side of the album: the doll wearing the Rolling Stones shirt.

412 c) Four days. The next project was the soundtrack for the film *Magical Mystery Tour.*

413 "Magical Mystery Tour"

414 Cynthia Lennon

415 a) Patti Harrison, George's wife

416 Their manager Brian Epstein died.

417 b) "I Am The Walrus"

418 b) Twenty-nine

419 James Taylor

420 False

421 "La Marseillaise," "In The Mood,"
"Greensleeves," and, according to one of the
horn players, snatches of Bach's Brandenburg
concerto.

422 True. Listen closely, and with the volume up as
high as you can stand it, during the seconds
right after the first "It's easy." He can also be *seen*
chewing gum while recording this track on the
televised documentary *The Beatles Anthology*.

423 b) "She Loves You." Mark Lewisohn, author of
The Beatles: Recording Sessions, identifies the
singer as John Lennon. However, furious
debates are likely to erupt over this contention,
generally initiated by dedicated Paul
McCartney fans.

424 True. It ran: "Yellow matter custard, green slop
pie, all mixed together with a dead dog's eye."

425 b) "'No You're Not,' Said Little Nicola."

426 a) The song: "All You Need Is Love." The
broadcast: "Our World," which took place on
June 25, 1967. Sheer speculation here, but the
occasional technical problems that mar the
song, including Harrison's muffed solo, may
have had something to do with the pressure of

performing live before a massive worldwide television audience.

427 John is on the bottom, of course, as the Walrus; above him, from left to right, are Paul, George, and Ringo.

428 "Magical Mystery Tour," "Your Mother Should Know," "I Am The Walrus," "The Fool On The Hill," "Flying," and "Blue Jay Way." In a rare instance of inspired U.S. repackaging of Beatles product, Capitol Records placed all these songs on Side One of the American LP release, and designated Side Two as the home of the Beatles' recent single releases that had not appeared on any LP: "Hello Goodbye," "Strawberry Fields Forever," "Penny Lane," "Baby You're A Rich Man," and "All You Need Is Love." Capitol then appropriated the British release's basic sleeve design and inner booklet, and it had itself an album—one that would eventually become the standard format for the songs in question back in the United Kingdom! Many listeners were puzzled, though, by the choice to include only the lyrics for Side One in the package; this was the result of Capitol's following the original layout of the British booklet.

429 Spaghetti—and plenty of it.

430 John Lennon

431 Dr. Joseph Crow

432 Prime Minister Harold Wilson may or may not have thought something along these lines, but he did not say this. If you guessed that this was the bogus quote, give yourself a pat on the back.

433 Kenneth Tynan, writing in *The Times*

434 Timothy Leary

435 Bob Dylan, to Paul McCartney, around the time of the release of *Sgt. Pepper*

436 *The Mirror* of London, in an editorial

437 Composer Ned Rorem, writing in *The New York Review of Books*

438 b) "Plenty Of Jam Jars"

439 c) Wonderlust

440 "Hello Goodbye"

fifteen

PAUL McCARTNEY
"CLUES"

Did a suave-looking replacement with a flair for writing songs like "Hey Jude" and "Lady Madonna" take over the deceased Paul McCartney's job in late 1966? No, but it made for good bong talk. (Answers begin on page 119.)

441 As part of the popular "Paul Is Dead" parlor game/group hallucination, it was fashionable to open the *Sgt. Pepper* album, point to the "O.P.D." inscription on Paul McCartney's uniform, and ominously inform anyone who would listen that the letters stood for "Officially Pronounced Dead." What do the letters really stand for?

  A. Ono: Predictor of Dissatisfaction
  B. Ontario Police Department
  C. Oswald Part of Design

442 John Lennon's lyric to "Glass Onion" identified Paul as the Walrus—and set off years of intricate guesswork. Eventually, the line was cited as a "clue" by passionate adherents of the Paul-Is-Dead school. What was Lennon's explanation for the true reason behind his inclusion of this line in the song?

  A. He was describing McCartney's favorite type of food.

  B. He was thanking McCartney for holding the group together.

  C. He was hoping to inspire Beatles fans to write obscure songs of their own.

443 Paul-Is-Dead "researchers" claimed that the Beatles had inserted the barely audible words "I buried Paul" at the very end of "Strawberry Fields Forever." With the release of *The Beatles Anthology 2* in March of 1996, Beatles fans were finally able to hear, quite distinctly, that John Lennon is saying no such thing. What nonsense phrase does Lennon actually drawl as the song fades out?

  A. "Cranberry sauce"

  B. "Hansbury's hot"

  C. "Not very large"

444 A certain carnation worn by Paul McCartney during the "Your Mother Should Know" section of the film *Magical Mystery Tour* set off a good deal of lurid speculation. What color was it?

445 The cover shot of the album *Abbey Road* features a Volkswagen Beetle with the license plate 28IF. Paul-Is-Dead sages solemnly asserted that the car's appearance was an intentional signal from the group that a particular Beetle—check that, Beatle—namely, Paul, would have been 28 *if* he had lived to the time of the album's release. What minor flaw mars this seemingly elegant piece of reasoning?

A. The plate should have read 27IF.
B. The plate should have read 26IF.
C. The plate bears a far more sinister message; in tiny letters, it says "Ignore Any References to Paul McCartney That Appear On This Cover."

446 A recording of the words "Bury my body" appears among the numerous other elements of the ending of the song "I Am The Walrus." This part of the track was often cited as evidence of another dark "clue" pointing toward Mr. McCartney's passage. Who is the actual source of this strange sentence?

A. Jim Morrison, who stopped by the studio while hallucinating on something or other.
B. George Martin, who supplied a tape-recording of random phrases, of which this happened to be one.
C. William Shakespeare

447 True or false: In 1969, United Press International released a story outlining the findings of a Florida audio expert with twenty years of scientific experience. The expert reported that he heard "three separate McCartneys" on various Beatles recordings, and expressed "reasonable doubt" that the same person was responsible for all the vocal tracks commonly held to be McCartney's.

448 True or false: On the *Imagine* album, John Lennon states straightforwardly that the Paul-Is-Dead theorists were right.

Answers

441 b) Ontario Police Department

442 b) In an interview shortly after the Beatles' breakup, Lennon explained that he used the line as a means of giving McCartney credit for holding the Beatles together over the years.

443 a) "Cranberry sauce"

444 It was black. Because the other Beatles were wearing red carnations, the flower was taken as an indication that its wearer had shuffled off this mortal coil. If *another* Beatle had been sporting a black carnation, the argument would no doubt have run that that particular Beatle was mourning McCartney's passing.

445 a) The supposedly deceased McCartney "would only have been" 27 at the time of the album's release.

446 c) William Shakespeare. The sentence comes from a line that can be found in Act Four, Scene Six of *King Lear*—line 251 in the Signet Classic edition, if you're keeping score at home. A radio performance of the play happened to be on while work was proceeding on "I Am The Walrus"; it was recorded and introduced to the song's rather chaotic final section. Larger chunks of the scene are clearly audible at various points. None of it has anything to do with Paul McCartney's fantastical early demise.

447 True. The researcher's current opinion on the evidence is unknown.

448 True. The caustic line from "How Do You Sleep" was, however, a withering assessment of McCartney's recent solo work, rather than an admission of an elaborate Beatles hoax.

sixteen

The Walrus Was... Ringo?

When asked, after the Beatles' breakup, about the "Paul-is-Dead" phenomenon, John Lennon insisted that it was all "made up. . . . People have nothing better to do than study Bibles and make myths about it, and study rocks. . . . " This common-sense approach may serve as the last word on the subject. Then again, it may not.

Closer examination of various Beatle album covers and tracks reveals that not one, but *all four* Beatles "died" in mysterious accidents in the early sixties, and were replaced by lookalike doppel-gangers just as the band's career took off. It just so happened that up to now we've missed all the mor-bid references to John, George, and Ringo that were liberally sprinkled throughout the (so-called) Beatles' recordings. The truth will out, however. Identify the Beatle whose pre-1965 "death" is revealed in each of the following clues. (Answers begin on page 125.)

449 Telltale "I may be asleep" lead vocal on "Blue Jay Way."

    A. Ringo Starr
    B. George Harrison
    C. Pete Best

450 Mutters "shoot me" repeatedly beneath guitar riff of opening track of *Abbey Road*.

    A. John Lennon
    B. George Harrison
    C. Stu Sutcliffe

451 Telltale "advice for those who die" lead vocal on "Taxman."

    A. Ringo Starr
    B. George Harrison
    C. Pete Best

452 Telltale "now it's time to say good night" lead vocal on "Good Night," serving as thinly veiled death metaphor after chaos and agony of "Revolution 9."

    A. Ringo Starr
    B. George Harrison
    C. George Martin

453 Telltale "they're going to crucify me" lead vocal on "The Ballad Of. . ." —oops, that would be giving it away, wouldn't it?

    A. Ringo Starr
    B. George Harrison
    C. John Lennon

kay, so much for the softballs. Now—on to the tough clues.

454 Appears smoking a cigarette on cover of *A Hard Day's Night*.

A. Stu Sutcliffe
B. George Harrison
C. John Lennon

455 Body "buried" in his hair on cover of *Revolver*.

A. Ringo Starr
B. George Harrison
C. John Lennon

456 Crucifix-like structure appears directly above his head on cover of *Please Please Me*.

A. Ringo Starr
B. Billy Preston
C. Pete Best

457 He's the only Beatle *not* sporting a Beatles haircut on the cover of *Please Please Me*, a clear sign of impostorhood.

A. Ringo Starr
B. Billy Preston
C. Pete Best

458 He's the only Beatle wearing black shoes on cover of *Abbey Road*.

A. Ringo Starr
B. George Harrison
C. John Lennon

459 Waxwork figure representing him on cover of *Sgt. Pepper's Lonely Hearts Club Band* appears wearing ominous black turtleneck, while those of other three Beatles have white shirts and ties.

A. Ringo Starr
B. George Harrison
C. John Lennon

460 On the cover of *Abbey Road,* he is standing in the middle of the lane with an oncoming vehicle approaching—and remember, we're in England, where people drive on the left.

A. Ringo Starr
B. George Harrison
C. John Lennon

461 He's the only Beatle wearing glasses with clear lenses (as opposed to sunglasses) on group photo that originally appeared on back of *Revolver* LP, a fashion choice reflecting a permanent passage to a higher spiritual state.

A. Ringo Starr
B. George Harrison
C. John Lennon

462 He's the only Beatle with head turned to back of camera on *A Hard Day's Night* cover.

A. Pete Best
B. George Harrison
C. Stu Sutcliffe

463 He's the only figure in black on cover of

Magical Mystery Tour. (Hint: He's dressed in *white* on *Abbey Road*.)

   A. Ringo Starr
   B. George Harrison
   C. John Lennon

464 Posed in arms-raised, Christ-on-the-cross position for cover of *Help!*

   A. Ringo Starr
   B. George Harrison
   C. John Lennon

465 Posed in slightly altered Christ-on-the-cross position, with both naked palms visible and outstretched, on cover of *Magical Mystery Tour.*

   A. John Lennon
   B. George Harrison
   C. Pete Best

466 Cover of one pre-breakup album inexplicably fails to include any photo or drawing of him.

   A. Ringo Starr
   B. George Harrison
   C. John Lennon

Answers

449 b) George Harrison

450 a) John Lennon

451 b) George Harrison

452 a) Ringo Starr

453 c) John Lennon, on "The Ballad Of John And Yoko"

454 b) George Harrison

455 a) Ringo Starr

456 a) Ringo Starr

457 a) Ringo Starr

458 a) Ringo Starr

459 a) Ringo Starr

460 c) John Lennon

461 c) John Lennon

462 b) George Harrison

463 c) John Lennon

464 c) John Lennon

465 b) George Harrison

466 a), b), and c) Ringo Starr, George Harrison, *and* John Lennon. For what it's worth, Paul McCartney qualifies, too. The album in question is *The Beatles* (a.k.a. *The White Album*).

seventeen

1968

The year everything happened, much of it to the Beatles. How many of the following questions about 1968 can you answer? (See page 141 for answers.)

467 Identify the speaker: "One night I went to bed with this guy and suddenly the next morning I see... [the] three relatives standing around staring at me."

468 "Yesterday" and "Eleanor Rigby" are examples of songs that feature musical and/or vocal contributions from only one Beatle: Paul McCartney. The group recorded only *one* song on which John Lennon is the only Beatle to appear. Which is it?

A. "Julia"
B. "Revolution 9"
C. "Everybody's Got Something To Hide Except Me And My Monkey"

469 Identify the John Lennon composition intended for inclusion in the *Yellow Submarine* film project, but removed from most prints of the picture.

A. "Revolution"
B. "Hey Bulldog"
C. "Give Peace A Chance"

470 Going to great lengths, part one: In 1968, the Beatles released their longest-ever single. Name it.

471 Going to great lengths, part two: The year 1968 also marked the appearance of the longest officially released Beatles album track. What was it?

472 True or false: Sergio Mendes and Brazil '66 scored a Top Ten U.S. hit in 1968 with their rendition of "The Fool On The Hill."

473 True or false: The Ray Conniff Singers scored a Top Ten U.S. hit in 1968 with their rendition of "I Saw Her Standing There."

474 In February of 1968, the Beatles landed in Rishikesh, India, with Maharishi Mahesh Yogi for an extended meditation retreat. Of the following people, who did *not* accompany them? Donovan, Mia Farrow, Prudence Farrow, Patti Harrison, Yoko Ono.

475 True or false: Bob Dylan had booked a flight to India, intending to accompany the Beatles on their retreat with Maharishi Mahesh Yogi, but he backed out at the last minute.

476 According to the televised documentary *The Beatles Anthology,* what brand of beans did

Ringo Starr, wary of strange food, bring in abundance to Rishikesh?

A. Heinz
B. B&M
C. Wonderwall

477 Which Beatle was the first to leave the Rishikesh retreat?

478 True or false: The song "Sexy Sadie" was once entitled "Maharishi."

479 Of what song released in 1968 would George Harrison later say, "Apart from the bit about the monkey, that was just what Maharishi used to always say"?

480 True or false: George Harrison set a chapter of the King James version of the Gospel of Matthew to music during the Beatles' stay in India, but the song was excluded from the Beatles' next LP.

481 All but one of the following songs were written in India. Spot the entry that doesn't belong. "The Continuing Story of Bungalow Bill," "Dear Prudence," "Mother Nature's Son," "The Inner Light," "I Will," "Ob-La-Di, Ob-La-Da," "Revolution 1."

482 True or false: John Lennon composed "Across The Universe" before leaving for India.

483 What was the first Beatles release on the Apple record label?

1968: THE MOVIE <u>YELLOW SUBMARINE</u>

ow much do you know about this full-length animated feature, which the Beatles regarded skeptically at first, but embraced enthusiastically when it proved to be a major critical and commercial success?

484 Before the Blue Meanies mount their assault on Pepperland, a huge statue honoring the word "KNOW" occupies a place of honor in an open field. What do the Blue Meanies do to this statue?

A. Paint it black
B. Destroy its first and last letters
C. Turn it upside down

485 Did the Beatles supply their own voices for the animated characters that bore their names in *Yellow Submarine*?

486 Whom does the Lord Mayor of Pepperland dispatch to get help from the outside world?

A. Sgt. Pepper
B. George
C. Fred

487 In the film *Yellow Submarine,* the Beatles encounter the Nowhere Man. What's his real name?

488 Of the following seas, which is *not* visited by the Beatles during the film *Yellow Submarine*?

A. Sea of Green
B. Sea of Holes
C. Sea of Time
D. Sour Milk Sea

489 One of the unforgettable visual creations of the *Yellow Submarine* film was a race of spindly fellows who went around dropping massive green apples on people. What were these unlikely creatures called?

490 All but one of the following nasties appear in the film *Yellow Submarine*. Spot the bad guy who doesn't belong: Dreadful Flying Glove, Skiing Snowman, Snapping Turks, Chief Blue Meanie.

491 In the film *Yellow Submarine,* which Beatle had a hole in his pocket?

492 True or false: Richard Lester directed *Yellow Submarine.*

493 Name the contributor to the *Yellow Submarine* screenplay whose later story of star-crossed Harvardians was a huge commercial success.

———————

494 True or false: In August of 1968, the Queen Mother wrote the Beatles a personal letter expressing her enjoyment at listening to the up-tempo rocker "Revolution."

495 True or false: During the tense sessions for the double album *The Beatles,* recording engineer Geoff Emerick left the project, explaining he could no longer work with the group.

496 True or false: During the tense sessions for the double album *The Beatles*, Ringo Starr left the project, explaining that he could no longer work with the group.

497 True or false: During the tense sessions for the double album *The Beatles,* producer George

Martin left the project, explaining he could no longer work with the group.

498 Who plays the dominant drum part on "Back In The U.S.S.R."?

499 The received wisdom regarding the double-disc set *The Beatles* is that it showcases a series of solo compositions, with the various Beatles primarily providing instrumental support to the composer (and lead vocalist) of a given song. This received wisdom is correct—with one exception. Name the single track on the album on which a singer other than the composer assumes a lead vocal. (No, "Revolution 9" doesn't count.)

500 At the conclusion of the hellacious "Helter Skelter," someone screams "I've got blisters on my fingers!" Who is it?

501 Identify the Beatle who plays saxophone on "Helter Skelter."

502 True or false: Jimi Hendrix sat in on the uproarious sessions for "Helter Skelter."

503 What is a helter-skelter?

    A. A type of English race car
    B. A type of English playground slide
    C. A type of English butcher knife

504 By the time Yoko Ono had entered his life, John Lennon was apparently feeling a little less desperate than he had during the period when he composed the song "Help!" For an instant between two songs on the double album *The Beatles,* someone (Ono?) can be heard saying

the word "pleh"—"help," spelled backwards.
Identify the two tracks that sandwich this
strange effect.

  A. "I Will" and "Julia"
  B. "I'm So Tired" and "Blackbird"
  C. "Revolution 9" and "Good Night"

505 During the song "Glass Onion," John Lennon
makes reference to the Cast Iron Shore. This is
one of (many) instances when Lennon came
across a real-life phrase that was simply too
good to leave out of a song. Where is the real
Cast Iron Shore?

  A. New York City
  B. Liverpool
  C. London

506 Name the violinist whose playing appears on
"Don't Pass Me By."

  A. Jack Fallon
  B. Jack Benny
  C. Louis Farrakhan

507 True or false: "Don't Pass Me By" was released
as a single in Scandinavia, where it reached the
#1 spot.

508 During the televised documentary *The Beatles
Anthology,* reference is made to the fact that the
1966 song "Paperback Writer," which features
extensive falsetto harmony work, was recorded
as a kind of response to the intricate vocals of
the Beach Boys. In 1968, the Beatles issued a
more direct tribute to/parody of the California
guys. What was it?

509 One-man band? Identify the songs on *The Beatles* that feature vocal and instrumental contributions from only one Beatle: Paul McCartney.

510 The Beatles recorded three "revolutionary" tracks in 1968. Can you name them, and place them in the order in which they began to be recorded in the studio?

511 The 1968 LP *The Beatles* marked the release of Ringo Starr's first solo composition. What was it?

512 True or false: This Ringo Starr composition once went by the working title "This Is Some Friendly."

513 There's something unusual about the bass line on the song "I Will." What is it?

514 What classic Beatles rocker began life as "I'm Backing the UK"?

515 What track appearing on the double-album set *The Beatles* did John Lennon lobby—unsuccessfully—to have issued as a Beatles single?

516 On the song "The Continuing Story Of Bungalow Bill," right after the children ask Bill whether or not it's a sin to kill, a distinctly non-Beatle voice shows up for a brief bit of lead vocal work. Whose voice is it?

A. Linda McCartney
B. Yoko Ono
C. Maureen Starkey

517 What track on the double album *The Beatles* begins with a strange conversation between Apple official Alistair Taylor and producer

George Martin regarding a forgotten bottle of claret?

518 For whom was the song "Dear Prudence" written?

A. Mia Farrow
B. Mia Farrow's sister
C. Ruth Gordon

519 Which Beatle plays bass on the song "Birthday"?

520 True or false: The original working title of "Why Don't We Do It In The Road" was "Shall We Procreate?"

521 Who sings lead on "Why Don't We Do It In The Road"?

522 Who was the chief composer of the song "Good Night," the final track on the double-disc set *The Beatles*?

523 Who plays the lead guitar solo on "While My Guitar Gently Weeps"?

524 How many takes did George Harrison put in on his song "Not Guilty," only to have it deemed unworthy of inclusion on the 1968 double album *The Beatles*?

A. 68
B. 74
C. 102

525 On what solo George Harrison record did "Not Guilty" eventually appear?

526 True or false: The song "The Continuing Story Of Bungalow Bill" is based on a real incident, a visit by an American hunter to Rishikesh, India, where the Beatles were engaged in a meditation retreat with Maharishi Mahesh Yogi.

527 True or false: The song "While My Guitar Gently Weeps" is based on a real incident in India in which a mysterious liquid was discovered oozing from George Harrison's acoustic guitar.

528 Identify all the previously released Beatles songs referenced in the song "Glass Onion."

529 In the song "Julia," a tribute to his late mother, John Lennon describes her by using the phrase "ocean child." To whom does this line also refer?

A. Queen Elizabeth II
B. Cynthia Lennon
C. Yoko Ono

530 One of the songs on *The Beatles* makes an unflattering assessment of Sir Walter Raleigh. Which one?

531 One of the tracks on *The Beatles* features the unexpected sound of the studio's echo tape-delay rewinding live during a take. What song is it?

A. "Honey Pie"
B. "Revolution 9"
C. "Martha My Dear"

532 One song included on *The Beatles* featured a preliminary take that ran for an incredible 27:11, the longest studio recording ever laid down by the band. Name it.

533 The song "Savoy Truffle" makes reference to another song that appears on *The Beatles*. Which one?

534 A guitar hero's fondness for chocolate supposedly inspired George Harrison to write the cautionary "Savoy Truffle." Who was it?

   A. Keith Richards
   B. Jimi Hendrix
   C. Eric Clapton

535 At one point in "Savoy Truffle," George Harrison opines that a particular dessert is good news. There's a double meaning at work in the phrase "good news." What is it?

536 The double-disc set *The Beatles* features three songs in a row in which animals are referenced in the title. Name them.

537 A set of four individual Beatle portraits was included with the two-disc set *The Beatles*. Identify the only Beatle in these photographs sporting no facial hair whatsoever.

538 True or false: Linda McCartney shot the four Beatle portraits included with the album.

539 The Beatles engaged in their longest continuous single studio session ever near the conclusion of work on *The Beatles*. How long did it run?

   A. Eighteen hours
   B. Twenty-four hours
   C. Thirty-six hours

540 True or false: The Beatles commissioned an artist to design the cover for the double-disc set *The Beatles* (a.k.a. *The White Album.*)

541 True or false: Furor over a "nude" shot of Paul McCartney included on the lyric sheet for *The Beatles* caused Capitol Records to airbrush out a segment of the photograph.

542 True or false: One of the titles considered for *The Beatles* was "A Doll's House."

543 True or false: John Lennon and Paul McCartney originally planned to release *The Beatles* as a single album.

544 A child inspired Paul McCartney to write "Hey Jude." Who was it?

   A. Julian Lennon
   B. Heather McCartney
   C. Zak Starkey

545 How many Grammys did the Beatles win in 1968, the year they released "Hey Jude," "Revolution," and the double-disc set *The Beatles*?

   A. Four
   B. Two
   C. Zero

546 True or false: Paul McCartney's vocal ad-libbing track can be heard *twice* during "Hey Jude."

547 What was the Beatles' only #1 single of 1968 in the United States?

548 The Beatles shot electrifying promotional films for their songs "Hey Jude" and "Revolution." Were these live performances?

549 A non-Beatle supplies the incandescent electric piano solo on the song "Revolution." Who is it?

   A. Nicky Hopkins
   B. Billy Preston
   C. Leon Russell

550 What sacred Taoist volume served as the inspiration for the lyrics of the song "The Inner Light"?

551 True or false: Faced with a losing business proposition in their Apple clothes boutique, the Beatles resolved the problem by giving away all the stock to passersby and closing down the operation.

552 Was John Lennon older or younger than Yoko Ono?

553 In December of 1968, John Lennon and Yoko Ono made an "appearance" at the Albert Hall, one that left photographers and other members of the news media more than a little bewildered. What was visually unusual about this early Lennon/Ono event?

554 True or false: John Lennon once called a meeting to inform his fellow Beatles, as well as a number of Apple insiders, that he, Lennon, was Jesus Christ reincarnated.

555 True or false: In 1968, John Lennon and Yoko Ono released a film entitled *Number Five* in which John's smiling face occupies the screen for fifty-two minutes.

556 True or false: In 1968, John Lennon and Yoko Ono released a thirty-two-minute film entitled *Stool*, which featured close-up shots of the feces of various luminaries.

557 True or false: Yoko Ono and Gordon Lightfoot recorded an early duet for Apple Records.

1968: CRYPTIC LYRIC ALERT

Identify the Beatles songs from this year that feature lyrics that reference:

558 A soap sculptor who consumes his own creations.

559 An automobile accident resulting in total baldness.

560 Barnyard animals in white starched shirts.

561 An eagle who picks at the singer's eye.

562 Contradictory pronouncements, within a single song, on the advisability of destruction as a means of social change.

563 Unambiguous dismissal of the advisability of destruction as a means of social change.

---

564 Name the young Paul McCartney protégé who scored an international hit with "Those Were The Days."

565 How old was this singer when "Those Were The Days" was released?

566 True or false: Paul McCartney had a hand in writing "Those Were The Days."

567 True or false: "Those Were The Days" supplanted "Hey Jude" at the top of the English hit parade.

568 The sessions for *The Beatles* concluded in October, 1968. What was the next album project the Beatles worked on?

Answers

467 Yoko Ono

468 a) "Julia"

469 b) "Hey Bulldog"

470 "Hey Jude," which runs for over seven minutes.

471 "Revolution 9," which runs for over eight minutes.

472 True

473 False

474 Yoko Ono

475 False

476 a) Heinz

477 Ringo Starr

478 True

479 "Everybody's Got Something To Hide Except Me And My Monkey." It's tempting to assume that the song's original title, when written in

India, could have been "Everybody's Got Something to Hide Except Maharishi." This song and "Sexy Sadie" offer intriguing insights on the India trip—and on John Lennon's creative process. Based on an obscene Lennon post-India studio sendup of the song that was to become "Sexy Sadie," many have concluded that the original version of that tune was a diatribe against their meditation instructor, hastily rewritten to avoid legal problems. Repeated listenings to both "Sadie" and "Monkey," however (as well as a certain instinctive trust in Lennon's ability to write impassioned songs about whatever cause he happened to be embracing at the moment) lead one to wonder whether or not these two songs might both have been composed as *tributes* to the Beatles' new spiritual leader, and then altered by simply revising the word "Maharishi" wherever it appeared. Certainly, replacing the phrases "me and my monkey" and "Sexy Sadie" with the word "Maharishi" in the lyrics of both tracks yields an intriguing Lennon pairing—complete with the author's trademark lapses into cynicism. The songs also seem to offer a taste of the adulation Lennon and the other Beatles showered upon the leader of the T.M. movement before their break with him.

480 False

481 "The Inner Light," which was released as the B side of "Lady Madonna" shortly after the Beatles left England for Rishikesh.

482 True. He did, however, compose the song *after* being initiated to Transcendental Meditation.

483 The single "Hey Jude," backed with "Revolution."

484 b) They destroy its first and last letters, leaving an ominous "NO" statue.

485 No. The actors who did the voices were Geoffrey Hughes as Paul McCartney; John Clive as John Lennon; Peter Batten as George Harrison; Paul Angelus as Ringo Starr.

486 c) Fred

487 Jeremy Hillary Boob, Ph.D. That last bit is pronounced "phd."

488 d) Sour Milk Sea

489 Apple Bonkers

490 The Skiing Snowman

491 Ringo Starr

492 False. The picture was directed by George Dunning.

493 Erich Segal, author of *Love Story*

494 True. The Royal Family had been presented with a special commemorative set of the first recordings on the Apple label; the Queen Mum responded to this gesture by sending a note in which she noted her pleasure at listening to them.

495 True

496 True. He was later coaxed into rejoining.

497 False

498 Paul McCartney; Ringo Starr, as noted above, had left the group, temporarily as it turned out.

499 "Good Night," a Lennon tune formally credited to Lennon/McCartney on which Ringo Starr sings lead

500 Ringo Starr

501 John Lennon, unlikely to be mistaken for Charlie Parker

502 False

503 b) A type of English playground slide

504 b) "I'm So Tired" and "Blackbird"

505 b) Liverpool. It's a waterfront area.

506 a) Jack Fallon

507 True

508 "Back In The U.S.S.R."

509 "Why Don't We Do It In The Road," "Martha My Dear," "Blackbird," "Wild Honey Pie," and "Mother Nature's Son."

510 Recording on the song that was eventually to become "Revolution 1" on the LP *The Beatles* began first; this led to the sound collage "Revolution 9," the next-to-last track on the same album. ("Revolution 9" originated from outtakes of "Revolution 1.") Finally, the band recorded the superb up-tempo rocker

"Revolution," which did not appear on the album.

511 "Don't Pass Me By"

512 True

513 It's not played by a bass guitar. It is, in fact, a vocal track laid down by Paul McCartney.

514 "Back In The U.S.S.R."

515 "Revolution 1." An up-tempo version of the same song, "Revolution," was featured as the B side of "Hey Jude."

516 b) Yoko Ono

517 "Revolution 9"

518 b) The song was written in India, while John Lennon was on retreat with Maharishi Mahesh Yogi. It was a plea to Prudence Farrow—sister of Mia, who was also in attendance on the retreat—to take a break from her seemingly endless meditation sessions and enjoy a beautiful day.

519 George Harrison

520 False

521 Paul McCartney

522 John Lennon

523 Eric Clapton

524 c) 102

525 *George Harrison*

526 True

527 False

528 In sequence: "Strawberry Fields Forever," "I Am The Walrus," "Lady Madonna," "The Fool On The Hill," and "Fixing A Hole."

529 c) Yoko Ono. The phrase is an English translation of her first name.

530 "I'm So Tired"

531 b) "Revolution 9." The sound begins at 3:25.

532 "Helter Skelter." The version in question—take three—has become something of a holy grail in rock history, representing one of the most elusive and sought-after of all "illicit" Beatles recordings. As of this writing, this reportedly raucous exercise remains unreleased.

533 "Ob-La-Di, Ob-La-Da"

534 c) Eric Clapton

535 "Good News" is the name of a particular brand of chocolates.

536 "Blackbird," "Piggies," and "Rocky Raccoon"

537 John Lennon

538 False. They were shot by John Kelly.

539 b) Twenty-four hours, starting at approximately 5:00 P.M. on October 16, 1968

540 True. The artist in question was Richard Hamilton, who also assembled the photo collage included on the reverse of the album's lyric sheet.

541 True. The photo in question features a decorously placed white strip down the middle that apparently didn't leave quite enough to the imagination to suit Capitol executives.

542 True

543 False. Despite suggestions from producer George Martin to this effect, the project was always conceived by the Beatles as a two-disc set, probably as a means of fulfilling contractual obligations to EMI.

544 a) It was John's son Julian, who was going through a rough patch as John and Cynthia Lennon were splitting up. The song's initial title was apparently "Hey Jules." However, it's worth noting that much of the record's lyric seems to be directed at an adult male who must make some sense of a dead relationship and commit to move on to a new one—a description that applies to both John Lennon and Paul McCartney during this period.

545 c) Not a one

546 True. The remarkable improvised vocal track bleeds through just a little on the early side. Listen carefully to the song, and you'll hear several faint traces of the very same vocal line that begins in earnest at 3:59. The most noticeable is the phrase "gotta break it," which seeps through at 3:35, long before it's meant to be heard at full volume at 4:27.

547 "Hey Jude"

548 Only the vocal tracks were.

549 a) Nicky Hopkins

550 The *Tao Te Ching*

551 True

552 Younger

553 The pair were concealed within a large white bag.

554 True. The meeting took place on May 18, 1968, and is detailed in Mark Hertsgaard's book *A Day In The Life*.

555 True. The original footage, three minutes in length, was slowed down for the film, which was also known as *Smile*.

556 False. They did, however, make a "documentary" that showcased the buttocks of famous personages.

557 False

558 "Happiness Is A Warm Gun"

559 "Don't Pass Me By"

560 "Piggies"

561 "Yer Blues"

562 "Revolution 1"

563 "Revolution"

564 Mary Hopkin

565 Seventeen

566 False. It was written by Gene Raskin.

567 True

568 *Let It Be,* which began life as *Get Back.* The final album would not, however, see the light of day until after the group completed work on, and released, *Abbey Road.*

eighteen
THE TWO SIDES OF JOHN LENNON

John Lennon was a songwriter occasionally given to composing tunes in matching pairs—sometimes over an extended period of time and sometimes in rapid succession. Here are some of those pairs, all recorded while Lennon was a Beatle unless otherwise noted. How many can you identify? (Answers appear on page 151.)

569 Name the "twin" songs that deal with the related topics of sleeping and insomnia.

570 Identify the two songs that incorporate, respectively, beginning-of-day and end-of-day greetings in their titles.

571 Two early Beatles songs with almost identical titles make up this next "twin" pairing. Identify the tracks, each of which appear to have been written chiefly by John Lennon, and each of which feature the word "Why" in the title.

572 Name the recordings that are slower and faster versions of the very same song.

573 "Part of me suspects I'm a loser," John Lennon told *Playboy* magazine in 1980, "and part of me thinks I'm God Almighty." Lennon wrote a pair of songs dealing directly with each half of this self-perception, one as a member of the Beatles, and one as a post-Beatles contribution to another artist's album. Name them both.

574 John Lennon wrote two songs for *Abbey Road* that feature lyrical echoes of *other* Beatles songs. Name them.

Answers

569 "I'm Only Sleeping" and "I'm So Tired"

570 "Good Morning Good Morning" and "Good Night"

571 "Tell Me Why" and "Ask Me Why"

572 "Revolution," released as the B side to "Hey Jude," and "Revolution 1," which appears on *The Beatles.*

573 "I'm A Loser" and "I'm The Greatest," which appears on *Ringo.*

574 "Sun King," which seems to adapt a line from "Here Comes The Sun" in its very first line, and "Come Together," which mentions a "walrus gumboot" reminiscent of "I Am The Walrus."

nineteen
1969

The Beatles showed unmistakable signs of coming apart at the seams in 1969. For that matter, so did just about everything else. We'll only be focusing on the Fab Four here, though. How many of the following questions can you answer? (See page 164 for answers.)

575 Talk about your advance release. The Beatles' first #1 single of 1969 in the United States preceded, by a full year, the album on which the composition would eventually appear. Identify the song.

576 The year 1969 saw the release of a Beatles song, composed by George Harrison, that sends up the Beatles' own music publishing company. Which song was it?

A. "It's All Too Much"
B. "Old Brown Shoe"
C. "Only A Northern Song"

577 Which Beatle abandoned the group during the *Let It Be* sessions, only to be coaxed back to finish the project?

578 Messrs. Harrison, Starr, and Lennon decided, in February of 1969, to take action to make sense of the group's tangled financial situation. Whom did they appoint to handle this job—over Paul McCartney's strenuous objection?

A. Allan Klein
B. Andrew Oldham
C. George Steinbrenner

579 On April 22, 1969, John Lennon legally changed his middle name. To what, and from what, did he change it?

A. From Berry to Peace
B. From Churchill to Nine
C. From Winston to Ono

580 On March 27, 1969, the last bachelor Beatle got married. Who was he? Whom did he wed?

581 Name the Lennon/Ono album that caused a scandal by featuring the two artists nude on the cover.

582 What compromise was arrived at to allow skittish distributors and retailers to sell this controversial—and musically undisciplined—disc?

A. Strategically placed strips of tape applied to strategic regions of the cover.
B. A legal requirement that anyone intending to purchase the album be forced to listen to it before doing so.
C. A brown paper bag.

583 What was the name of the officer who oversaw the 1969 raid of George Harrison's residence, resulting in Harrison's arrest for possession?

A. Norman Pilcher
B. Enoch Powell
C. Denny Laine

584 True or false: Also arrested at Harrison's residence by this officer was former teen idol Frankie Lymon.

585 True or false: The officer in question ended his law-enforcement career in disgrace following a conviction related to planting evidence.

586 In 1969, the Beatles released an LP on which the first song of Side One featured a lead vocal by Ringo Starr. Identify it.

587 While recording "Across The Universe," the Beatles recruited the aid of Lizzie Bravo and Gayleen Pease, who supplied the backing vocals. Who were Bravo and Pease?

A. Members of the local Transcendental Meditation group.
B. Professional singers who had worked with Dave Mason.
C. Fans who were hanging out near the studio.

588 Name the Dutch hotel at which newlyweds John Lennon and Yoko Ono talked in their beds for a week.

589 The song "The Ballad Of John And Yoko" mentions that its twin protagonists eat chocolate cake in an unusual place. Where?

590 Where were John Lennon and Yoko Ono married?

591 "The Ballad Of John And Yoko" makes reference to a number of acorns contained in a sack. How many of these acorns did John and Yoko employ during their 1969 wedding-for-peace campaign?

592 What were the acorns for?

593 How many Beatles attended the recording sessions for the song "The Ballad Of John And Yoko"?

594 Who plays the drums on "The Ballad Of John And Yoko"?

595 Name the movie studio where some of the scenes for the movie *Let It Be* were shot.

596 Midway through the *Get Back/Let It Be* sessions, the Beatles adjourned to Apple Studios, where a friend of John Lennon's who specialized in electronics had promised a host of breathtaking advances in recording technology. In the event, these advances never materialized. Identify the legendary Apple character who promised the Beatles 72-track recording technology, but dropped the ball big time.

  A. "Magic" Alex Mardas
  B. Mal Evans
  C. Peter Brown

597 Name the 1969 film in which Ringo Starr appeared with Peter Sellers.

598 In 1970, the Beatles would fracture over, among other things, Paul McCartney's insistence on recording and releasing a solo record, *McCartney*. In 1969, however, another Beatle released a single *while fronting another band,* a single that cracked the Top Twenty in the United States. Name the Beatle and the single.

599 At the conclusion of the song "It's All Too Much," George Harrison tosses off a line from a 1966 hit by a group named after a river familiar to Beatles fans. Name the song.

1969: CRYPTIC LYRIC ALERT

Identify the Beatles songs from this year that feature the following:

600 A man who waits in line for his lover's top lip.

601 Counterfeit notes—or are they Sunday comics?—passed along instead of hard cash.

602 The description of all reality as "birthday cake."

603 An armchair that radiates disease.

604 An "equation" between love given and love received—perhaps meant as a theological conclusion related to encounters with the Almighty after death(?).

——————

605 "Come Together," the song that opens the *Abbey Road* album, was a title not entirely unfamiliar to attentive Beatle fans. On what noteworthy occasion had John Lennon used the phrase during 1969?

606 The opening line of John Lennon's "Come Together" matches a line from an old Chuck Berry tune. Can you name the song?

607 True or false: The song "Come Together" was initially intended as a campaign song for Timothy Leary—who was pondering a run for governor of California during the Ronald Reagan years, and whose campaign slogan was "come together."

608 A recording artist who got his first big break from the Beatles recorded a song whose title showed up as the first line of one of the most memorable tracks on *Abbey Road*. Name the artist and the song.

609 The sessions for *Abbey Road* were marked, for a time, by one Beatle's absence—due to an automobile accident. Name the Beatle.

610 Do octopuses really build underwater gardens?

611 Identify the four *Abbey Road* tracks on which John Lennon makes no contribution whatsoever. (Three appear on Side Two.)

612 George Martin described one of the songs on *Abbey Road* as "in some ways. . . one of the best songs ever written." What song was he talking about?

A. "Something"
B. "Come Together"
C. "Here Comes The Sun"

613 Can you name all the songs in *Abbey Road*'s extended, two-part Side Two medley? (Hint: The first one is "You Never Give Me Your Money.")

614 There are two songs on the album *Abbey Road* to which Ringo Starr makes no contribution. One is an exquisite harmony piece that requires no drums; the other is a Paul McCartney acoustic number. Name them.

615 True or false: After "Yesterday," George Harrison's "Something" is the Beatles composition that has been most often recorded by other artists.

616 True or false: During early rehearsals of the song "She Came In Through The Bathroom Window," the Beatles recorded a version in which Paul's declaration that he'd quit the police department and gotten himself a job was followed by the words "Bloody 'bout time, too!"

617 True or false: In 1969, John Lennon arranged for a double bed and an overhanging microphone to be installed in the Abbey Road studios for Yoko Ono's use.

618 True or false: During the fadeout of the song "Maxwell's Silver Hammer," Paul McCartney incorporates a whispered, barely audible slur on the Manson family.

619 What famous American entertainer described the song "Something" as "the greatest love song of the past fifty years"?

A. Frank Sinatra

B. Dean Martin

C. Sammy Davis, Jr.

620 What non–Beatle plays organ on the *Abbey Road* tracks "Something" and "I Want You (She's So Heavy)"?

A. Billy Preston

B. Nicky Hopkins

C. Leon Russell

621 Which two Beatles play the repeating, over-dubbed lead guitar riffs that conclude "I Want You (She's So Heavy)"?

622 True or false: The hard-to-understand words of the song "Sun King" on *Abbey Road* are a series of thinly veiled personal attacks by John Lennon against various members of London's Metropolitan Police Department—rendered in Italian.

623 What event inspired the song "She Came In Through The Bathroom Window"?

A. A robin that flew into Paul McCartney's window.

B. A burglary through Paul McCartney's bath-room window.

C. A hallucination involving a bathroom win-dow.

624 It's mentioned in the song "Mean Mr. Mustard," which appears on *Abbey Road*, that the creepy title character has a sister. What does she do for a living?

625 During the *Get Back* sessions, John Lennon performed an earlier version of "Mean Mr. Mustard," one in which Mr. Mustard's sister had a different first name. What was her—more alliterative—appellation in this incarnation of the song?

A. Sally
B. Cindy
C. Sissy

626 Who wrote the original lyrics Paul McCartney adapted for the song "Golden Slumbers"?

A. William Shakespeare
B. Thomas Dekker
C. Francis Bacon
D. Edward de Vere

627 What word in that original "Golden Slumbers" lyric did McCartney replace with "darling"?

628 The album *Let It Be*, because it was the Beatles' final release before breaking up, is often mistaken for the group's farewell statement. In fact, that record consisted almost entirely of material recorded *before* the tracks appearing on *Abbey Road*. Identify the aptly named track on *Abbey Road* that marks the Beatles' real "curtain call"—recorded in the final days of the band's incarnation as a studio foursome.

629 On that track, as the Beatles line up for their collaboration-ending curtain calls, Ringo Starr unleashes one of his two formally released drum solos as a Beatle. What song contains the other one?

630 After Ringo's drum solo, the remaining Beatles exchange guitar solos for three alternating cycles of exuberant jamming. In what order do the guitar-toting Beatles play as they bid their fans—and their own group—farewell?

631 What was the last day all four Beatles showed up within the walls of the Abbey Road studios at the same time?

    A. June 1, 1969
    B. August 20, 1969
    C. December 12, 1969

632 The album *Abbey Road* won one Grammy. In what category did it win?

633 Name the photographer who shot the *Abbey Road* cover.

    A. Linda McCartney
    B. Iain Macmillan
    C. Richard Avedon

634 True or false: The Volkswagen featured on the cover of *Abbey Road* was sold at auction by Sotheby's in 1986.

635 What was the original proposed title for the album eventually released as *Abbey Road*?

    A. *You're Really Beginning To Get On My Nerves*
    B. *Everest*
    C. *Four Men*

636 Identify the permanent members of the Plastic Ono Band, which was formed in 1969.

637 In October of 1969, one of the Beatles began

work on a new solo album, produced by George Martin. Which one?

638 What was the songwriting credit for the single "Give Peace A Chance"?

639 In what city was "Give Peace A Chance" recorded?

   A. Montreal
   B. Amsterdam
   C. London

640 A future Academy Award–winning actress reportedly recorded a protest song entitled "John You Went Too Far This Time" after John Lennon and Yoko Ono appeared nude on the cover of a 1969 album. Who was the pseudonymous protester?

   A. Meryl Streep
   B. Sissy Spacek
   C. Faye Dunaway

641 True or false: Among the reasons cited by John Lennon in returning the MBE he had received from the Queen in 1965 was the poor chart performance of his recent single "Cold Turkey."

642 True or false: Canadian leader Pierre Trudeau met personally with John Lennon and Yoko Ono in 1969 to discuss the Lennons' peace campaign.

643 True or false: In 1969, John Lennon and Yoko Ono released a forty-two-minute documentary film entitled *Self-Portrait* in which John's penis is shown, in slow motion, as it rises to erection.

644 What was the date of the Beatles' final photo shoot—regarded by many as their last day together as a group?

  A. June 3, 1969
  B. August 22, 1969
  C. December 22, 1969

645 True or false: The Beatles' official 1969 Christmas fan club recording featured a story from John Lennon about "two balloons called Jock and Yono" who "battled on against overwhelming oddities, including some of their beast friends."

646 True or false: The former Linda Eastman, who wed Paul McCartney in 1969, is related to the Eastmans of Eastman Kodak fame.

647 True or false: In a 1969 interview, George Harrison maintained that he, too, was the Walrus.

648 True or false: The Beatles recorded an unreleased (and much sought-after) collection of improvisatory tunes with Doors singer Jim Morrison in 1969.

649 In December of 1969, John Lennon and Yoko Ono paid for a series of billboards and full-page advertisements that blared the headline "WAR IS OVER!" to observers. What four words appeared in much smaller type beneath this supremely eye-catching Vietnam-era headline?

650 In December of 1969, John Lennon proposed a new designation for the upcoming year. What was it?

A. Peace
B. One
C. Nine

651 What was the Beatles' last #1 single of 1969 in the United States?

Answers

575 "Get Back"

576 c) "Only A Northern Song." Bearing all the earmarks of a song written out of legal commitment, rather than artistic inspiration, this track may represent a high-water mark for cynicism in the recording industry unmatched until the release of *Monty Python's Contractual Obligation Album*.

577 George Harrison

578 a) Allan Klein. Harrison, Starr, and Lennon combined to override McCartney's objections to Klein. Eventually, the three Beatles who supported Klein would sign a contract with Klein, but McCartney would not. Much legal wrangling and chaos within the group can be traced to this event.

579 c) It had been Winston; he changed it to Ono.

580 Paul McCartney; he married Linda Eastman.

581 *Unfinished Music #1—Two Virgins*

582 c) The album was concealed in a brown paper bag.

583 a) Detective-Sergeant Norman Pilcher

584 False

585 True, according to the televised documentary *The Beatles Anthology,* which reported that Pilcher received a four-year sentence from Mr. Justice Malford Stevenson. Stevenson pronounced: "You poisoned the wells of criminal justice, and you set about it deliberately. What is equally bad is that you betrayed your comrades in the Metropolitan Police, a force which commands the respect of the civilized world."

586 *Yellow Submarine.* The song was, of course, "Yellow Submarine."

587 c) Bravo and Pease were fans who made a habit of hanging out near the Beatles' studio. The two young ladies' contributions are less evident on the Beatles' *Let It Be* album than they are on *Past Masters Volume Two.*

588 The Amsterdam Hilton

589 In a bag. Not *from* a bag, mind you, but *in* a large white sack. This was a real-life John and Yoko media stunt, a typical piece of Lenono play circa 1969.

590 In Gibraltar, a colony of the British crown located near Spain, on March 20, 1969

591 Fifty

592 The couple announced that they would offer the acorns to major world leaders as a gesture for peace.

593 Only John Lennon and Paul McCartney

594 Paul McCartney

595 Twickenham Studios

596 a) "Magic" Alex Mardas

597 *The Magic Christian*

598 John Lennon and the Plastic Ono Band reached #14 in the States with "Give Peace A Chance."

599 "Sorrow," by the Merseys

600 "Old Brown Shoe"

601 "You Never Give Me Your Money"

602 "It's All Too Much"

603 "Come Together"

604 "The End"

605 While recording "Give Peace A Chance"

606 "You Can't Catch Me"

607 True

608 The artist: James Taylor. The song: "Something In The Way She Moves."

609 John Lennon, who was involved in a crash in Scotland

610 Yes

611 "Here Comes The Sun," "Maxwell's Silver Hammer," "Her Majesty," and "Golden Slumbers." (The source of the personnel accounts for these songs is Ian MacDonald's exhaustive *Revolution in the Head*.)

612 c) "Here Comes The Sun"

613 Act One: "You Never Give Me Your Money," until crickets and chimes lead to . . . "Sun King," until languid polylingual crooning yields to . . . "Mean Mr. Mustard," until acoustic power chords usher in . . . "Polythene Pam," until hypercharged Lennon studio chatter brings us to . . . "She Came In Through The Bathroom Window." Intermission. Act Two: "Golden Slumbers" until brusque drumbeat starts up . . . "Carry That Weight" the last note of which serves as the first note of . . . "The End."

614 "Because" and "Her Majesty"

615 True

616 True. The enthusiastic puncturer of McCartney's lyric was, of course, the ever-acerbic John Lennon.

617 True

618 False

619 a) Frank Sinatra

620 a) Billy Preston

621 John Lennon and George Harrison

622 False. The words are vintage Lennon gobbledy-gook.

623 b) A young fan's burglary of the McCartney home through that entryway.

624 She works in a shop.

625 a) Sally. The line in which her name appears sounds a bit cooler this way; presumably the name change was made in deference to developing a sense of continuity during the extended medley that occupies most of Side Two of the album.

626 b) English dramatist and pamphleteer Thomas Dekker—born 1570, died 1632. Considering the similarly fanatical, hallucinatory intent of the various partisans in the "Paul-Is-Dead" and "Shakespeare-Didn't-Write-His-Own-Plays" campaigns, it's remarkable that this fact has not yet been spun into some thesis under which Dekker actually composed *all* of McCartney's songs. . . or, alternatively, that Shakespeare was replaced by the "lookalike" Dekker after a serious horseriding accident caused the Bard of Avon's early demise and cut short a promising playwriting career.

627 "Wantons"

628 "The End"

629 "Birthday"

630 Paul McCartney, George Harrison, John Lennon

631 b) August 20, 1969. The occasion: Mixing work for the *Abbey Road* LP.

632 As Best Engineered Recording

633 b) Iain Macmillan, working from a sketch by Paul McCartney

634 True

635 b) *Everest*

636 John Lennon and Yoko Ono

637 Ringo Starr; the album was *Sentimental Journey*. Paul McCartney's later *McCartney* was self-produced.

638 Lennon/McCartney

639 a) Montreal

640 b) According to author Nicholas Schaffner, the artist in question was Sissy Spacek, who released the recording under the name "Rainbo."

641 True. Although the reference to "Cold Turkey" was a throwaway line in a more serious message calling attention to British complicity in the U.S. war in Vietnam, among other issues, it served as fodder for yet another round of unflattering press stories centering on Lennon.

642 True

643 True. No, really. They did. As Dave Barry is wont to note, dear readers, I am *not making this up.*

644 b) August 22, 1969

645 True

646 False

647 True

648 False

649 "If you want it"

650 b) One. "Everyone who's into peace," Lennon announced, "will regard the New Year as Year One A.P. for 'After Peace'. All of our letters and calendars from now on will use this method."

651 "Something," with "Come Together" on the flip side.

twenty

SPOT THE
WANNABE GROUP!

Any band as big as the Beatles can expect to spawn an imitator or two. How many of the following can you identify? (Answers begin on page 172.)

652 This made-for-television batch of pseudo-Beatles scored major hits like "Last Train To Clarksville" and "I'm A Believer." What was the group called?

653 One of the Beatles' most important direct competitors released an embarrassingly obvious rip-off of *Sgt. Pepper's Lonely Hearts Club Band* that served as one of the artistic low points of that band's career. Identify the album and the band.

654 In 1970, this band took a Paul McCartney song into the U.S. and UK Top Ten listings—and made some people wonder whether or not it was the Beatles recording under another name. Identify the group and the song.

655 What seventies band, rumored to be the Beatles themselves recording under a strange name inspired by a science fiction film, released a song called "Calling Occupants Of Interplanetary Craft"?

656 Identify the down-on-his-luck artist who assembled an unfortunate disc misleadingly entitled "Best Of The Beatles."

657 This Beatles-reminiscent seventies combo revived Capitol's familiar sixties-era multicolored record labels, and were the focus of a brief nineties revival when one of their songs showed up in a Winona Ryder movie. Name the band.

658 One of the early American hits from this Beatlesque nineties British combo—probably the best of the Beatles-modeled bands—had a title inspired by a solo George Harrison LP. Name the group and the song.

Answers

652 The Monkees

653 The album: *Their Satanic Majesties' Request.* The group: the Rolling Stones.

654 Badfinger, with "Come And Get It"

655 Klaatu

656 Sad but true: Pete Best

657 The Knack. The song in question was "My Sharona."

658 Oasis. The song: "Wonderwall."

twenty~one

1970

The Beatles were finished as a foursome, but as 1970 began, most of the world didn't realize it. How many of these questions from the group's breakup year can you answer? (See page 183 for answers.)

659 In February of 1970, John Lennon and Yoko Ono cut their hair. Why?

660 Between the releases of *Abbey Road* and *Let It Be,* another Beatles LP was unveiled, one that reached the #2 position in the United States. Name it.

661 On *Let It Be's* "For You Blue," George Harrison laughingly refers to a legendary blues quitarist. Whom does he invoke?

  A. Eric Clapton
  B. Elmore James
  C. Ravi Shankar

662 What Beatle plays the slide guitar solo in "For You Blue"?

663 On the LP *Let It Be,* Ringo briefly bails out of the number "Dig A Pony" just as it's starting. Why?

    A. He has to blow his nose.
    B. He's distracted by his wife, Maureen.
    C. He's meditating and misses the count-in.

664 The *Let It Be* album features, unexpectedly, an unmistakable songwriting collaboration between John Lennon and Paul McCartney, the two having focused almost exclusively on solo compositions in the period following their sojourn to India. Name the half-and-half song that combined their talents once again and appears on this album.

665 John Lennon repeats the phrase "Jai Guru Deva Om" during the chorus of a song that appears on *Let It Be*. Identify the song, and translate the strange-sounding phrase.

666 To whom does the line about "Mother Mary" in the song "Let It Be" refer?

    A. Mary Wells
    B. Mary McCartney
    C. The Virgin Mary

667 What American keyboard player helped the Beatles out on *Let It Be*?

    A. Ray Charles
    B. Leon Russell
    C. Billy Preston

668 What Beatle plays bass on the song "The Long And Winding Road"?

669 What Beatle plays bass on the song "Let It Be"?

670 What Beatle plays lead guitar on the song "Get Back"?

671 What was the B side of the single "The Long And Winding Road"?

    A. "Everybody's Got Something To Hide Except Me And My Monkey"
    B. "Let It Be"
    C. "For You Blue"

672 What was the Beatles' final pre-breakup single release in Britain?

673 The Beatles' first #1 U.S. single of 1970 faced a competing song on the American charts that had been released by a Beatle working as a solo artist! Identify both songs.

674 True or false: An early attempt at the song "Free As A Bird" appears in the film *Let It Be*.

675 True or false: An early attempt at the song "Band On The Run" appears in the film *Let It Be*.

676 True or false: An early attempt at the song "Maxwell's Silver Hammer" appears in the film *Let It Be*.

677 True or false: An early attempt at the song "Octopus's Garden" appears in the film *Let It Be*.

678 How many of the twelve tracks on *Let It Be* feature orchestral overdubs?

    A. Seven
    B. Five
    C. Three

679 Before Phil Spector completed work on what would become the *Let It Be* album, engineer Glyn Johns had a go at salvaging the tapes from the early 1969 sessions, and prepared an album called *Get Back* that the Beatles decided against releasing. Whose version contains more tracks from the live Beatles performance that took place on the Apple rooftop—Glyn Johns' or Phil Spector's?

680 True or false: The original title of "Two Of Us" was "Four Of Us Chasing Paper."

681 Which of the Beatles attended the world premiere of *Let It Be* in New York City?

682 As the B side to one of their 1970 singles, the Beatles served up an unruly comedy record entitled "You Know My Name (Look Up The Number)." The strange track, which features an intriguing combination of silly voices, low-rent hambone, and diaphragmatic emissions, can be heard on the *Past Masters Volume Two* CD. Which Beatle has named this unlikely track as his favorite Beatles song of all?

683 What gave John Lennon the idea for the oft-repeated title phrase of the song "You Know My Name (Look Up The Number)"?

A. A telephone company slogan
B. A screaming fan who was being led away from his mansion by police
C. A business meeting at Apple

684 Who plays alto saxophone on "You Know My Name (Look Up The Number)"?

  A. John Lennon
  B. Charlie Parker
  C. Brian Jones

685 Name the last Beatles single release of 1970.

686 In 1970, Paul McCartney caused quite a stir by insisting on releasing his solo album, *McCartney,* in competition with the Beatles' *Let It Be.* Name the session musicians who contributed to *McCartney.*

1970: THE ROOFTOP CONCERT

How much do you know about the top-of-the-building performance that is the highlight of the film *Let It Be?*

687 True or false: Before the Beatles decided to give their Apple rooftop concert, they were considering appearing in concert at an ancient amphitheater as the finale to the *Get Back* project.

688 Where did the concert actually take place?

689 How many songs from the rooftop session feature a George Harrison lead vocal?

690 What songs did the Beatles perform during the rooftop session?

691 During the film *Let It Be,* someone can be seen

kneeling in front of John Lennon with a clip-board during "Dig A Pony." Why?

A. Lennon was unsure of the lyrics.
B. Lennon was making a political statement by incorporating an antiwar message on the clipboard for the film.
C. There was an important message from Yoko waiting for him.

692 At the conclusion of the Beatles' rooftop rendition of "One After 909," John Lennon lets loose with a line from another song—one perhaps not previously associated with the Beatles *oeuvre*. Identify it.

693 True or false: The version of "Get Back" heard at the end of *Let It Be* is taken from the rooftop concert.

694 Whose red coat is Ringo Starr wearing during the rooftop performance?

695 Whose fur coat is John Lennon wearing during the rooftop performance?

696 As the *Let It Be* album concludes, Paul McCartney says something that sounds like "Don't smoke." What is he really saying?

A. "That smells"
B. "House mold"
C. "Thanks, Mo"

697 Why did the rooftop concert end?

A. The Beatles' hands got too cold to play.
B. The electricity gave out.
C. The police showed up and put a halt to things.

698 Identify the former Beatle who was the first to score a #1 single in the U.S. once the group announced its breakup.

699 Identify the former Beatle who was the first to score a #1 album in the U.S. once the group announced its breakup.

700 In late 1970, John Lennon let it all hang out in an extensive series of interviews in which he discussed the Beatles, their breakup, his relationship with Yoko Ono, and a variety of other topics. Who conducted the interviews?

A. James Reston
B. Jann Wenner
C. Andy Warhol

701 What periodical first published them?

A. *The New York Times*
B. *Rolling Stone* magazine
C. An extremely early issue of *Spin*

702 What was the name of the book they were turned into? (Hint: The book title made punning reference to the memoirs of a deposed world leader.)

703 True or false: In 1970, the Beatles released an album entitled *The Beatles Again*.

704 True or false: On a 1970 episode of "The Brady Bunch," Marcia Brady dreams of going out on a date with Paul McCartney.

705 True or false: Paul McCartney's 1970 *McCartney* LP features a shot of the solo artiste, free at last, and picking his nose.

1970: CRYPTIC LYRIC ALERT

Identify the Beatles songs that feature the following ambiguous references from the year 1970.

706 A puzzling account of wet dreams, unfettered hair, and droopy socks.

707 People chasing paper and getting nowhere.

708 The ominous union of the CIA, the FBI, and the BBC.

709 A hearty welcome to a mysterious—and distinctly chintzy—nightclub.

———

710 What was the first single release by Ringo Starr after the formal announcement that the Beatles had broken up?

A. "You're Sixteen"
B. "It Don't Come Easy"
C. "Beaucoups Of Blues"

711 What was the first single released by George Harrison after the formal announcement that the Beatles had broken up?

A. "Wah Wah"
B. "Awaiting On You All"
C. "My Sweet Lord"

712 What was the first single released by John Lennon and the Plastic Ono Band after the formal announcement that the Beatles had broken up?

A. "Imagine"

B. "How Do You Sleep"
C. "Mother"

713 At one point on his *Plastic Ono Band* LP, John Lennon does the rock 'n' roll equivalent of Orson Welles' destroying-the-room scene from *Citizen Kane,* lashing out at every emblem of illusion, humbug, and misplaced trust in external authority he can think of: Elvis, the Bhagvad Gita, the Bible, the I Ching, and, yes, the Beatles. What is the title of this song?

714 During this song, Lennon tells the listener that he among the entities in which he no longer believes is "Zimmerman." Who or what is Zimmerman?

715 Shades of Alanis Morissette! As though leaving any feather unruffled might constitute a compromise of his artistic integrity, John Lennon made a point of using the word "fuck" not once, but twice, during another impassioned song that appears on *John Lennon/Plastic Ono Band.* Name it.

716 A great deal of *John Lennon/Plastic Ono Band* was composed while Lennon was undergoing a controversial form of therapy. Identify it.

A. Aromatherapy
B. Methadone therapy
C. Primal therapy

717 True or false: *John Lennon/Plastic Ono Band* was part of a two-record release; its companion album was *Yoko Ono/Plastic Ono Band.*

THE BATTLE ROYAL

This was not a good time for Beatles fans. In 1970, and in the year that followed, they had to watch the two senior partners of their favorite band engage in public, bitter, and increasingly personal attacks upon each other, notably through a famous series of letters and interviews appearing in *Melody Maker* magazine, but also by means of their own solo records. Who is the author of each of the remarks below: John Lennon or Paul McCartney?

718 Regarding his former partner's solo work: "Muzak to my ears."

719 "So what if I live with straights? I like straights."

720 In response to the self-posed question, "Do you miss the other Beatles and George Martin?": "No."

721 "Join the Rock Liberation Front before it gets *you.*"

722 In response to the self-posed question, "Did you enjoy working as a solo?": "Very much. I only had me to ask for a decision, and I agreed with me."

723 "We'd just sign the paper and hand it to the business people and let them sort it all out. That's all I want now. But [he] won't do it. Everybody thinks I am the aggressor. But I'm not, you know. I just want out."

724 "[He] hasn't left [the band.] I sacked him."

725 "[They] are not cool in what they are doing."

726 "If we're *not* cool, *what does that make you?*"

727 "Have you ever thought that you might *possibly* be wrong about something?"

728 ". . . you can't just 'sign a bit of paper.'"

Answers

659 In order to help black activist Michael X raise money for his Black House center by auctioning off the hair.

660 *Hey Jude.* This compilation of single tracks previously unreleased in LP format features, on its front and rear covers, photographs from the Beatles' very last photo session as a group.

661 b) Blues guitar player Elmore James

662 John Lennon

663 a) He has to blow his nose. Producer Phil Spector, apparently in search of as many moments of *audio verite* as possible, immortalized the moment on disc.

664 "I've Got A Feeling"

665 The song is "Across the Universe"—previously included on a charity album, and spruced up for mainstream release by Phil Spector. The phrase "Jai Guru Deva Om" translates roughly as "Hail Guru Dev, Om." Guru Dev was the teacher of Maharishi Mahesh Yogi, with whom the Beatles studied Transcendental Meditation.

666 b) Paul McCartney's mother, whose name was Mary, and who died in his youth. In 1968, Paul had a dream in which she appeared and offered messages of comfort; hence the song.

667 c) Billy Preston

668 John Lennon—and none too expertly, either

669 John Lennon

670 John Lennon

671 c) "For You Blue"

672 "Let It Be," which came out in March of 1970

673 "Let It Be," which entered the American charts in March of 1970, reached #1; it was in direct competition with John Lennon's "Instant Karma," which made its first chart appearance at the end of February, peaked at #3, and remained on the U.S. charts for thirteen weeks.

674 False

675 False

676 True

677 True

678 c) Three: "The Long And Winding Road," "I Me Mine," and "Across The Universe." It's an arguable point, but of these tracks, only the first can be said to be truly "over the top," and "The Long And Winding Road" presents a special case, in that its basic track represents something less than the Beatles' best instrumental work. Disparaged for years, Phil

Spector's work on this album is perhaps most notable for its tactful editing and "cleanup" of the recordings in question, a feat accomplished on nine of the album's twelve tracks without resorting to heavenly choirs or massive echo, two "wall of sound" hallmarks. In late 1970 John Lennon, not exactly in a Mantovani phase of his career, weighed in with a generally positive assessment of Spector's work.

679 Phil Spector's. See Mark Lewisohn's *The Beatles: Recording Sessions,* page 169, for a breakdown of which song ends up where.

680 False

681 None of them

682 Paul McCartney (see the interview with him that appears in Mark Lewisohn's *The Beatles: Recording Sessions).* The selection is an understandable one from McCartney's point of view: this bizarre number was pulled from the vaults for reworking in April of 1969, and it served as an unmistakable—if increasingly rare—reminder of the good feeling between Lennon and McCartney that had been notably absent in the just-concluded *Get Back* sessions.

683 a) A slogan exhorting the use of the London telephone directory: "You know the name, look up the number."

684 c) Brian Jones of the Rolling Stones

685 "The Long And Winding Road." The song was the group's final #1 single release to date.

686 There was only one. Paul McCartney played every instrument for every track of the album.

687 True. During the televised documentary *The Beatles Anthology,* Neil Aspinall mentions that this was being actively considered.

688 Atop the Beatles' Apple recording studios in London.

689 None of them

690 "Get Back" (three times), "Don't Let Me Down" (twice), "I've Got A Feeling" (twice), "The One After 909," "Dig A Pony," and (extra credit time) "God Save The Queen"—not the Sex Pistols' classic, which would not be released for some time, but a comparatively straight-ahead rendition of the national anthem performed while an engineer changed tapes.

691 a) Lennon was uncertain of the lyrics, a not uncommon state of affairs. The televised documentary *The Beatles Anthology* provides a wealth of superb live performances, any number of which feature muffed Lennon vocals. Perhaps the band should have incorporated the clipboard device a few years earlier!

692 "Danny Boy"

693 False. Although producer Phil Spector would have preferred listeners to conclude otherwise, the rooftop chat and laughter with which the *Let It Be* album concludes has no real connection to the *studio* rendition of the song that immediately preceded it.

694 His wife Maureen's

695 His wife Yoko Ono's

696 c) "Thanks, Mo"—acknowledging the appreciative and vocal applause of Ringo Starr's wife, Maureen.

697 c) The London police arrived and put a halt to the proceedings.

698 George Harrison, with "My Sweet Lord"

699 Paul McCartney, with *McCartney*

700 b) Jann Wenner

701 b) *Rolling Stone* magazine

702 The book was called *Lennon Remembers*, a canny twist on the clandestinely taped memoirs of former Soviet leader Nikita Khrushchev, which were entitled *Khrushchev Remembers*.

703 True. This was an alternate title for the singles-compilation LP otherwise known as *Hey Jude*.

704 False. Marcia was more of a Davy Jones admirer.

705 True

706 "I've Got A Feeling"

707 "Two Of Us"

708 "Dig It"

709 "You Know My Name (Look Up The Number)"

710 c) "Beaucoups Of Blues"

711 c) "My Sweet Lord"

712 c) "Mother"

713 "God"

714 This is the given last name of Bob Dylan, who adopted a new performing name in honor of the poet Dylan Thomas. It is interesting that Lennon decides not to launch an "I don't believe in Dylan" missile during "God," opting instead to settle for a subtler comment on the personal hypocrisy of altering one's name in the name of mass acceptance. Clearly, Dylan's *work* still meant a great deal to Lennon. It's worth noting, too, that Lennon appears to have taken a dim view of stage names in general. When an author wrote that Lennon had assumed the name "Johnny Silver" during the early Beatle years, he submitted a humorous, but earnest, denial of this.

715 "Working Class Hero"

716 c) Primal therapy, championed by Dr. Arthur Janov. The method culminates in the recovery of traumatic early memories, leading to a supposedly cleansing round of howling on the part of the patient. The influence of the "Primal Scream" is clearly evident on *John Lennon/Plastic Ono Band*.

717 True.

718 John Lennon

719 Paul McCartney

720 Paul McCartney

721 John Lennon

722 Paul McCartney

723 Paul McCartney

724 John Lennon

725 Paul McCartney

726 John Lennon

727 John Lennon

728 John Lennon

twenty~two
CHATTER DURING SONGS

dentify the song or songs that feature the follow-ing strange remarks, all *spoken* rather than sung, and all culled from various Beatles releases. Extra credit: Identify the speaker! (Answers begin on page 191.)

729 ". . . Charles Hawtry and the Deaf Aids. Phase One, in which Doris gets her oats."

730 "Full speed ahead, Mr. Boatswain."

731 ". . . Made [for] John Lennon."

732 "Believe me, darling."

733 ". . . I feel my finger on your trigger. . . "

734 "Better believe it!"

735 "Well, do next time."

736 "We're going home. . . "

737 "Rosetta. . . "

738 "One more time. . . "

739 "Step right this way!"

740 "The Queen says no to pot-smoking FBI members."

741 "Sweet Loretta Fart, she thought she was a cleaner, but she was a frying pan."

742 "All together now. . . everybody. . . "

743 "Elmore James got nothing on this, baby."

744 "Enough of that. . . "

745 "I'm gonna get that boy."

746 "Hold it!"

747 "Oh, *look out*. . . "

748 "Don't look at me, man, I already have grand-children."

749 "You become naked."

750 "Let's hear it for Dennis!"

751 "Good night everybody. . . "

752 "Home. H-O-M-E."

753 "Bye!"

754 "I hope we passed the audition."

Answers

729 John Lennon, at the beginning of "Dig A Pony"

730 Paul McCartney, on "Yellow Submarine"

731 John Lennon—or at least a computer-assisted recreation of him—weighs in with this at the end of "Free As A Bird."

732 Paul McCartney, "Oh! Darling"

733 John Lennon, "Happiness Is A Warm Gun"

734 Ringo Starr, at the *very* end of "Lovely Rita." Also: Paul McCartney, as "Two Of Us" concludes. ("You'd better believe it.")

735 The "song" is "Revolution 9"; the speaker is producer George Martin, taking part in a (barely audible) conversation at the very beginning of the track, shortly after "Cry Baby Cry" fades out on McCartney's "Can you take me back. . . "

736 Paul McCartney, at the end of "Two Of Us"

737 Paul McCartney; the word appears just before "Get Back" on the album *Let It Be.*

738 George Harrison, "Piggies"

739 Paul McCartney, "Magical Mystery Tour"

740 The remark appears between "The Long And Winding Road" and "For You Blue" on *Let It Be.* The speaker is John Lennon.

741 This sample of free-spirited John Lennon parody appears before the track "Get Back" on *Let It Be.*

742 Paul McCartney, "All You Need Is Love"

743 The song: "For You Blue." The speaker: George Harrison.

744 Paul McCartney, "Hey Jude." The entire phrase: "Enough of that, Jude!"

745 Paul McCartney, during "Rocky Raccoon"

746 Ringo Starr, during the count-in to "Dig A Pony"

747 This John Lennon outburst appears between the songs "Polythene Pam" and "She Came In Through The Bathroom Window" on *Abbey Road*.

748 Paul McCartney, during the free-spirited conclusion of "Hey Bulldog"

749 The speaker is Yoko Ono, and the track is "Revolution 9."

750 John Lennon, the enthusiastic Master of Ceremonies on "You Know My Name (Look Up The Number)"

751 Ringo Starr's whispered conclusion to "Good Night"

752 John Lennon can be heard far, far in the background of "Ob-La-Di, Ob-La-Da," saying this after one of Paul McCartney's "Home sweet home" lines. You may need a good pair of headphones to hear this one.

753 John Lennon, during the Paul McCartney count-off that begins "Sgt. Pepper's Lonely Hearts Club Band (Reprise)." Alternate answer: Paul McCartney, who says "Good-bye" at the end of "Two Of Us."

754 John Lennon's remark from the conclusion of the Beatles' 1969 rooftop concert appears at the end of the *Let It Be* album.

twenty~three

The "Free As A Bird" Video: It's Even More FAAB When You Hit the "Pause" Button

Remember the stunning video that accompanied the 1995 release of "Free As A Bird"? Pull out your videotape of the first evening of the ABC special "The Beatles Anthology," and fast-forward to the end. It's time to play a little game of "how-many-song-references-did-you-get." Important note: The author makes no claim that *all* of the song references appearing in the video are discussed here! (See page 200 for answers.)

755 Shortly after the video begins, the Beatles are seen walking with a group of men along the Liverpool docks. What's the weather like—and what song is being referenced by the weather?

756 Later in the video, we see a young boy wandering through a certain park with a strangely familiar name. What song does this image recall?

757 Not long afterwards, the video presents us with the first of several shots of young children running. Identify the *two* Beatles songs these images connect to.

758 On a busy street, a delivery man is seen near an egg truck. What song does he represent?

759 You'll need a slow-motion pass through the next section of the video for this one. Shortly after the above-referenced delivery man's appearance, four strange figures can be seen standing atop a distant building. . . for a couple of brief frames. Look to the upper left quarter of your screen for them. Who are they? What song are they meant to remind you of?

760 What song does the nurse represent—and why does she look directly at the camera?

761 What song does the barber represent?

762 After some cameo appearances by figures familiar to those generally acquainted with the political scene in Britain in the sixties (and particularly acquainted with the Profumo scandal), we see Ringo jumping out of a doorway. To what song does this image refer?

763 Shortly after Ringo's modest leap, we see a couple—John and Yoko?—engaged in a serious makeout scene in the back of a car. What appealingly direct love song leaps to mind?

764 At the time of the "Free As A Bird" video's first broadcast, the three posters that whizzed past around this part of the film must have seemed like random collages of various photographs and drawings of the Beatles. What are they really?

765 Not long after we see those strange posters, we catch a glimpse of a cake in a bakery window. What two songs does this cake make reference to?

766 Shortly after George Harrison exits his car, we see a metal nameplate on the front of the building he walks into. What title of a Beatles song appears on that nameplate?

767 Not long after this, a line of police officers is seen stationed near a crowd at an automobile accident. What two songs do the accident scene and the officers, respectively, represent?

768 Once the "bird" who serves as our camera leaves the accident scene, it heads toward one of the video's most puzzling references—for Americans, at least. Most Beatle fans in the U.S. had to stop and think for a while about the deliberate, has-to-mean-*something* shot of what appeared to be a lighthouse. British fans had a much easier time identifying this structure and the song it represented. What was it?

769 An object is seen soaring in the sky immediately after we encounter that lighthouse-like construction. What is it, and what song is it meant to suggest?

770 Look! There's a ladder leading into an open window. Identify the song this scene represents.

771 See the sunflowers? Pretty big ones, aren't they? What song do they illustrate?

772 Watch out! Here come a bunch of children wearing pig masks. There are puddles on the street. Identify not one, not two, not three, but four songs that can be connected to this scene.

773 Pull out the remote again—you'll need the slow-motion button to make out what's on the window of the apartment we're soaring into. Can you identify it? Do you remember the song it connects to?

774 You're now in the rather cramped apartment of a fellow who's pecking away at a typewriter. Who is he?

775 The typist's desk calendar—what does it say, and what song does it reference?

776 On a table in front of John Lennon—a houseguest of our busy typist—is a newspaper. To what song does this periodical refer?

777 As we emerge from the clutter of the typist's apartment, secure in the knowledge that we have not yet unearthed its many mysteries, we notice from the window that some repair work is being done on a nearby building. What kind of work are the men doing on the rooftop?

778 Who is that blue individual who appears near the workers for an instant?

779 On the street below the workmen, a man is walking a dog. What sort of dog is it? What song does the dog connect to?

780 What's the deal with the strange designs on the taxicab that pulls up in front of the apartment building?

781 Why does the young woman get into that oddly decorated cab?

782 A huge portrait is being carried across a street. Whose image does it bear?

783 Déjà vu! Someone just reappeared after only a few seconds' absence. Who is he?

784 To a dedicated Beatles fan, the sight of John and Yoko waltzing across the street in the "Free As A Bird" video brings to mind two Beatles songs, each featuring a George Harrison lead vocal. Can you name them both?

785 Don't get too distracted by John and Yoko's dancing. Off in the distance, a strange bus is speeding past. Can you identify it?

786 Déjà vu all over again! There's Ringo at a table. What is he holding? What movie/song does it remind you of?

787 Now we're in the presence of an unusual procession that features attendants galore, a matronly woman carrying a small satchel, and an elephant. What song do these images represent?

788 Step in and take your place among the most eclectic gathering of party guests ever captured on video. The attendees include Brian Epstein (who can be seen wrapping a scarf around his neck), an Indian holy man, various important-looking literary types, and a cardboard cutout featuring the body of James Dean set beneath the head of a Beatle who left the group before it attained any significant commercial success. Why, it's as though the Beatles were introducing us to everyone who'd ever had an important influence upon them! That sure would be a cool idea for an album cover, wouldn't it? Just in case we missed the point, the sequence incorporates a shot of a prop from the *Sgt. Pepper* photo shoot. Which one?

789 The next section of the "Free As A Bird" video takes place in a graveyard. This portion of the video references the songs "Lady Madonna" (note the moving statue), "Martha My Dear" (see the sheepdog speeding past?), and "Eleanor Rigby" (a gravestone bearing her name is clearly visible, as is a clergyman walking away). Directly across from the cemetery we see a twisting road in the distance ("The Long And Winding Road"), a young woman carrying a suitcase ("She's Leaving Home"), and a whimsical Paul McCartney cavorting atop a hill ("The Fool On The Hill"). What do these songs have in common, and why are they set in or near a cemetery?

790 Warning: If there is a nastier, subtler hidden visual clue in the entire video than the one you're about to see, this man hasn't come across it yet. As we pan past the cavorting Paul McCartney and into a cluster of trees, we see a reference to the song "Blackbird." What is it?

791 On a familiar-looking street, we see a woman in uniform dutifully inspecting a line of parked cars. Who is she? Where is she?

792 You know, when you think about it, the entire "Free As A Bird" video can be said to be a reference to a single Beatles song. Which one?

793 As the "Free As A Bird" video concludes, we see a man on a music-hall stage playing what appears to be a ukulele. What connection does the ukulele have with John Lennon's younger years?

Answers

755 "Rain"

756 "Strawberry Fields Forever"

757 Both "I Am The Walrus" and "Lady Madonna" feature the line "see how they run."

758 "I Am The Walrus." The delivery man is, of course, an "egg man."

759 They're the four Beatles, as pictured on the cover of the album *Help!* The reference is to the song of the same name.

760 She represents the "pretty nurse" who sells "poppies from a tray" in "Penny Lane"; she looks directly at the camera because she "feels as if she's in a play" but "is, anyway."

761 "Penny Lane" again. Together with the nurse and a few other references hereabouts, it's hard not to conclude that this segment of the video is meant to be set under the blue suburban skies of that song.

762 "A Hard Day's Night," inasmuch as it is a clip from the film of the same name.

763 "Why Don't We Do It In The Road?"

764 The album covers of the three *Anthology* double-CD sets.

765 The cake, which features the words "Happy Birthday" and the number "64," is meant to recall both "Birthday" and "When I'm Sixty-Four."

766 "Doctor Robert"

767 "A Day In The Life"—remember the driver who blew his mind out in a car?—and "I Am The Walrus," which references a group of policemen in a row. Lennon's presence in the crowd is a tip-off.

768 A children's playground slide, known as a "helter skelter" in England. The going-up, coming-down images associated with this staple of British playgrounds form the core of Paul McCartney's lyric for the decidedly unchild-like rocker of the same name.

769 A kite; the song is "Being For The Benefit Of Mr. Kite!"

770 "She Came In Through The Bathroom Window," of course. If you replay this particular section a few times in slow motion, you'll spot the woman's foot being drawn into the building.

771 "Lucy In The Sky With Diamonds"—these sunflowers are, after all, flowers of yellow and green that would tower over one's head.

772 In addition to the above-referenced "see how they run" double link that leads the image to both "I Am The Walrus" and "Lady Madonna," there are two *more* songs to snag here. The most obvious, of course, is "Piggies." The obscure—and final?—link in this particularly complex image points toward the song "Rain," with its people who run and, yes, hide their heads when the weather gets rainy.

773 It's a lizard perched on a windowpane, but it's only visible for a fraction of a second. The song in question is "Happiness Is A Warm Gun."

774 He's the Paperback Writer, of course. In addition to being a representative of a song title— and a relatively easy one to identify, at that—he is also the occupant of an apartment that probably incorporates more elliptical Beatles references than any other abode on the face of the earth. Even dedicated students of the "Free As A Bird" video have despaired of identifying every clue scattered about this maddeningly intricate residence.

775 It features the number eight, for "Eight Days A Week."

776 "A Day In The Life." The fact that newspaper stories are mentioned throughout the song is probably enough to make the connection, but the clincher is the hard-to-read headline, which will, after you've run it back and forth on slow motion for a while, make reference to a breaking piece of news from Blackburn, Lancashire. Lennon's presence in this shot leads many students of the video to believe that we're in the presence of a good many additional song references hereabouts, and there is a strong case to be made for the presence of a glass onion on top of the television set. This image, however, like so many in the Paperback Writer's chaotic abode, is excruciatingly difficult to fix with any certainty. The maybe/maybe-not status of a reference to "Glass Onion," an oblique song about oblique song references, would only be fitting in this supremely dense, hard-to-figure section of the "Free As A Bird" video.

777 They're "Fixing A Hole."

778 The Chief Blue Meanie, from the film *Yellow Submarine*

779 A bulldog. The song in question is "Hey Bulldog."

780 They're newspapers. It's a "newspaper taxi," from "Lucy In The Sky With Diamonds."

781 Because "She's Leaving Home," of course. Another—and apparently different—home-leaving young lady appears later in the video. As you may have already gathered, such repetitions prevent us from enjoying any sense of satisfaction at having "crossed a song off the list." Just to keep us on our toes, the Fabs have inserted multiple visual references to the same song at various points of the "Free As A Bird" video.

782 Chairman Mao's. If the people carrying it had any sense, they'd realize they ain't gonna be making it with anyone, anyhow. The reference is to the songs "Revolution" and "Revolution 1." For the record, another portrait that looks very much like Mao's is shown on the window of the Paperback Writer's apartment. Perhaps the dual reference is meant to correspond to the two versions of the song—or to Lennon's infamous "in/out" ambivalence about the advisability of using destruction as a political tool? Truth be told, there's a lot of in-and-out hereabouts.

783 The Chief Blue Meanie from *Yellow Submarine.* It's worth noting that his unlikely occupancy of a hole in the street recalls that of another Beatles film villain, the eccentric cult leader played by Leo McKern in *Help!*

784 "I'm Happy Just To Dance With You" and "I Me Mine." The film clip in question is from a portion of the film *Let It Be,* in which the pair waltz to "I Me Mine." Some have suggested that the dancing-Lennons segment of the "Free As A Bird" video also relates to "Why Don't We Do It In The Road," but there are two problems with this interpretation. A: Any number of things are done in the road during the video, and not all of them can be meant to connect to that song. B: "Why Don't We Do It In The Road" is not about dancing. It is about sex.

785 It's the "Magical Mystery Tour" bus.

786 Ringo is holding a camera, as he did in *A Hard Day's Night.*

787 "The Continuing Story Of Bungalow Bill."
Bill, you will remember, was in the habit of
going hunting with his elephant, and of bring-
ing along his mother just in case there were
any accidents. It's not surprising, then, that she's
clutching a doctor's bag.

788 The drum. The Beatle featured in this
sequence is Stuart Sutcliffe.

789 They all feature lead vocals from, and were primarily composed by, Paul McCartney, whom a
good many fans once believed to have died
and been replaced by a slick-sounding replacement.

790 Be prepared to stare for a while to catch this
one, even in slow-mo. As the foliage comes
into view, a bird takes off—and its now-"broken" wings split in two and keep on flying. A
real toughie, but it's there. Don't be surprised if
this one eludes you for a while.

791 She is Rita, the heroine of "Lovely Rita." She
is, of course, walking down Abbey Road,
miraculously reconfigured to its mid-1969
appearance, when it served as the setting for
the cover shot for *Abbey Road*.

792 "Flying"

793 John Lennon's mother Julia was an enthusiastic
player of the instrument. During the television
documentary *The Beatles Anthology*, Paul
McCartney recalls watching her play by his
friend's side.

twenty-four
The Breakup
Years... and Beyond

ow many of the following questions from the post-breakup period can you answer? (See page 222 for answers.)

794 John Lennon, Paul McCartney, George Harrison, and Ringo Starr all released post-Beatle singles that went to #1 in the United States. Name the first for each to hit the top spot in America.

795 Identify the speaker: "As soon as I touched the Beatles, boom, they broke up. But it happened before. The Righteous Brothers, the Crystals, and the Ronettes. Give 'em to [me], and they'll break up."

796 Within three years of the Beatles' breakup, each solo Beatle had scored in the United States with either a #1 (for Paul, John, and George) or #2 (for Ringo) LP. Name the first solo album to reach the slot in question for each artist.

797 What song on George Harrison's *All Things Must Pass* LP was the subject of a bitter copyright dispute?

798 In 1971, John Lennon released a Christmas-season single credited to "John Lennon and Yoko Ono Plastic Ono Band With the Harlem Community Choir." What was it called?

799 What was John Lennon's first solo album to be released after the announcement of the breakup of the Beatles?

800 In the Beatles song "Glass Onion," John Lennon vaguely denies being the Walrus. He does it again, and without equivocation, during one of the most memorable songs of his solo career. Name it.

801 On his breakthrough album *All Things Must Pass,* George Harrison included a song called "Apple Scruffs." What is an Apple scruff?

802 One of the highlights of George Harrison's *All Things Must Pass* album is a tune he cowrote with Bob Dylan. Can you name it?

803 The George Harrison song "Wah-Wah," which appears on *All Things Must Pass* was inspired by an argument Harrison had with someone. Whom?

804 Who produced George Harrison's landmark solo album *All Things Must Pass*?

805 What was the first single released by Paul McCartney after the formal announcement that the Beatles had broken up?

806 What was the official reason cited for the refusal of John Lennon's U.S. visa application?

807 Who originally prompted George Harrison to "do something" about the extraordinary constellation of natural and man-made calamities that overtook the tiny country of Bangladesh in the early seventies?

808 The Beatles did not reunite during the Concert for Bangladesh, although rumors had been circulating that they might. Something else almost as magical happened, though. What was it?

809 Which former Beatles were in attendance at the Concert for Bangladesh?

810 One of the following performers *didn't* appear during the Concert for Bangladesh. Which one? Eric Clapton, Mick Jagger, Billy Preston, Leon Russell, Ravi Shankar.

811 Three Beatles songs written by George Harrison appear on the *Concert For Bangladesh* album. Identify them.

812 What was the name of the single George Harrison quickly recorded and released, with proceeds to benefit Bangladesh relief fund?

813 True or false: *The Concert For Bangladesh* reached the #1 spot in the U.S. album charts.

814 What famous producer personally oversaw the recording of the live Bangladesh concert?

815 On his *Ram* album, Paul McCartney may have taken some ill-advised potshots at his former partner John Lennon in songs such as "Too Many People," "3 Legs," and "Dear Boy." The vaguely unnerving lyrics of "Too Many People" told of an unidentified person who managed to blow his lucky break, and enjoined listeners to avoid falling under the spell of those who spent too much time "preaching practices." The words of "3 Legs" pointedly address someone whom the singer had thought to be his friend, but who let him down. And "Dear Boy" expresses less-than-convincing sympathy for an unnamed acquaintance who never really appreciated how much he'd missed. What decidedly less subtle lyrical assault from the album *Imagine*, released a few months later, did Lennon unleash on McCartney?

A. "Jealous Guy"
B. "How Do You Sleep"
C. "Crippled Inside"

816 As though unsure whether his song had gotten across his point about his feelings regarding his former partner, John Lennon packaged a special postcard with his album *Imagine* that showed him in a barnyard posture very similar to that of Paul McCartney on the cover of *Ram*. Instead of a ram, though, Lennon poses with a different animal. Identify it.

817 Two insects are visible on the rear cover of Paul McCartney's 1971 album *Ram*. What kind are they, and what are they doing?

818 There is a private(?) message to Linda McCartney to be found on the cover of *Ram*. What is it?

819 With what 1971 song from the LP *Wild Life* did McCartney issue a subdued defense to the barrage of attacks from his former partner?

820 In the early seventies, the studio at which the Beatles recorded most of their material formally changed its name to Abbey Road Studios, thanks to the worldwide fame the album *Abbey Road* had bestowed on the location. What was the formal name of this studio before the name change?

821 Political activism to go, please: This former Beatle raised more than a few eyebrows when he released a 1972 single entitled "Give Ireland Back To The Irish." Name him.

822 What labored, dutifully leftist 1972 album from John Lennon failed to rise any higher than #48 on the U.S. album charts?

823 What nationally respected publication did the cover of this album parody?

824 True or false: Alarmed at the former Beatle's political influence, Senator Strom Thurmond wrote a confidential memo in 1972 suggesting that President Nixon's Justice Department take action to deport John Lennon.

825 True or false: President Richard Nixon reluctantly vetoed a plan, hatched by his "Plumbers" unit, to sell tainted LSD to John Lennon.

826 During Paul McCartney's 1972 and 1973 European concert tours, how many songs did he perform from the Lennon/McCartney repertoire?

827 In 1973, Paul McCartney released a catchy single about, well, sex that was promptly banned by the BBC. Name it.

828 Name the Paul McCartney song composed expressly for a James Bond film.

829 On his 1973 album *Mind Games,* John Lennon included a brief track entitled "Nutopian National Anthem." What were the lyrics?

830 The 1965 hit "Wooly Bully" popularized the phrase "L7"—which meant, roughly, "squaresville." (Get it? L on the left? 7 on the right? A square?) In 1973, Paul McCartney released a song whose title was meant to describe the acme of coolness, and it boasted a clever title that paid tribute to that old Sam the Sham and the Pharoahs tune. What was the record called?

831 What seventies David Bowie hit quotes a line from "A Day In The Life"?

   A. "Young Americans"
   B. "Fame"
   C. "Suffragette City"

832 Paul McCartney headed to, of all places, Lagos, Nigeria, to record parts of the post-Beatle album that would salvage his tarnished reputation among the critics—and stand, to this day, as probably the sharpest entry in the solo Fab album sweepstakes. Name the breakthrough album from Paul that spent 116 weeks on the U.S. Top 200 list, won an Album of the Year award from *Rolling Stone* magazine, and featured, in a *Pepper*-like touch, a cover bearing the unexpected faces of actors James Coburn and Christopher Lee.

833 True or false: Actor Dustin Hoffman suggested that Paul McCartney write a song based on painter Pablo Picasso's last words—and McCartney did, more or less on the spot.

834 True or false: After years of putting up with Beatles releases that were several tracks shorter than the corresponding British LPs, American McCartney fans finally turned the tables in 1973. McCartney's album was released with an *additional* track appearing on the U.S., and not on the UK, version.

835 True or false: In 1974 John Lennon was ejected from the Troubador nightclub in Los Angeles for disrupting the performance of a man with whom he had recorded a hit record in the '60s.

836 What was the name of the solo album on which John Lennon got back to where he once belonged—and appeared on the cover, in a pre-Beatlemania photo, sporting a black leather jacket.

837 True or false: Anne Murray recorded a cover of a Beatles song that reached the Top Ten in the United States in 1974.

838 True or false: David Bowie, having worked with both men, arranged sessions for a bizarre "supergroup" recording of a still-unreleased Christmas record; it featured harmony work from Bowie himself, John Lennon, and Bing Crosby.

839 True or false: George Harrison held a face-to-face meeting with President Gerald Ford at the White House in 1974.

THE "NINE" THING

The number nine looms large in John Lennon's legend, with regard to his work both as a Beatle and as a solo artist. How many of the following nine questions can you answer?

840 Lennon's ninth solo album, released in the ninth month of 1974, yielded a single that featured the number nine in the title and peaked at #9 on the American charts. Although it has been curiously overlooked in the years since its composer's death, this dreamy, gauzy single is a worthy successor to "Strawberry Fields Forever," and certainly one of Lennon's most exquisite solo achievements. Name it.

841 What nine foreign-sounding syllables, supposedly inspired by a dream of Lennon's, appear in this song?

842 A Lennon solo album from 1973 contains nine letters in its title. Can you name it?

843 Lennon's album of classic rock covers also contained nine letters in its title. What was it called?

844 John Lennon's birthday features the number 9. What is it?

845 Nine words make up the most important phrase in one of Lennon's most important antiwar songs. Can you recall the phrase?

846 One of the earliest songs Lennon cowrote with Paul McCartney appears on the group's *Let It Be* album, and uses the number nine twice in its title. Can you name it?

847 A work profoundly influenced by Yoko Ono, and appearing on the double-disc set *The Beatles,* prominently features the number nine. What is it called?

848 A certain letter appears nine times in the complete, legal names of John and his wife. Which one?

---

849 Identify the songs John Lennon performed onstage with Elton John in late November of 1974 at New York's Madison Square Garden.

850 John Lennon appeared with Elton John on this occasion as the result of losing a bet. What was it?

851 Someone special visited John Lennon backstage after his appearance with Elton John. Who was it?

852 In 1975, John Lennon cowrote a song that David Bowie took to #1. Name it.

853 In 1975, John Lennon released, as a single, a cover of a rock 'n' roll standard. Much later, the original version of the song in question served as the theme of an extremely popular film directed by Rob Reiner. Name the tune.

854 Do you remember the name of the band that backed up John Lennon for the concert that eventually became the album *Live In New York City*?

855 One of the technicians who had worked with the Beatles as a (very youthful) tape operator during the *Let It Be* and *Abbey Road* sessions emerged years later as a recording artist to be reckoned with in his own right. Name him.

856 Something unusually important happened on John Lennon's thirty-fifth birthday. What was it?

857 In what year was the Beatles' legal partnership dissolved?

858 True or false: Faced with mounting problems related to his disputes with U.S. immigration officials, John Lennon asked the Queen of England for a formal pardon for his 1968 marijuana conviction.

859 True or false: John Lennon played guitar on a post-breakup remake of a Beatles tune that was a major hit in the United States.

860 True or false: Ringo Starr scored a Top Ten American hit with an anti-drug tune.

861 True or false: Paul McCartney's band Wings released, as a single, a recording of "Mary Had A Little Lamb."

862 True or false: In 1975, Ringo Starr released, as a single, a song entitled "Oo-Wee."

863 True or false: In 1972, John Lennon released, as a single, a song entitled "Ono (Here I Go Again)."

864 True or false: In 1974, George Harrison released a song entitled "Ding Dong, Ding Dong."

865 What Ringo Starr solo LP featured two U.S. #1 singles?

866 Of George Harrison, John Lennon, and Paul McCartney, which former Beatles contributed musically to the above-mentioned Ringo Starr LP?

867 True or false: Ringo Starr's screen career has included a film in which he portrays Frank Zappa.

868 True or false: Ringo Starr's screen career has included a low-budget, underground production of *Who's Afraid of Virginia Woolf?* in which Starr portrays Nick.

869 True or false: Ringo Starr's screen career has included the role of the Pope.

870 True or false: Ringo Starr directed a documentary focusing on the band T Rex.

871 When was John Lennon finally granted the right to live in the United States on a full-time basis?

872 What January 1977 event marked Lennon's moment of high triumph over the departed Blue Meanies of the Nixon Administration who had fought against his living in the U.S.?

873 In 1977, Paul McCartney and Wings released a song that ended up becoming his biggest-ever British hit. The song made no splash to speak of in the U.S., though, and was even omitted from McCartney's 1987 *All The Best* greatest-hits collection. What was the song, and on what American LP was it first released?

874 Someone happened to have a low-budget tape recorder on during a 1962 Beatles Hamburg performance. Name the LP, released in 1977, on which this sub-bootleg-quality material appeared.

875 Name the up-tempo two-disk collection, consisting entirely of previously released Beatles material, that roared to the #2 spot on the U.S. album chart in 1977.

876 In the '70s, Capitol Records released a catchy Beatles song that had never been issued as a single. The single in question was a Top Ten U.S. hit, despite the fact that it had been released—and quite well known—for nearly ten years. Name the song.

877 What was the name of the Paul McCartney lookalike played by Eric Idle in the hilarious seventies pseudodocumentary, *The Rutles: All You Need Is Cash?*

878 Which Beatle had a cameo role in *The Rutles: All You Need Is Cash?*

879 Which of the following was *not* a song featured in *The Rutles: All You Need Is Cash?* "Cheese and Onions," "Hold My Hand," "Let's Be Natural," "Piggy In The Middle," "Zzzzzzz."

880 What was the name of the successful Broadway show featuring Beatles soundalikes and trippy sixties-era light shows?

881 Who played Mr. Kite in the film *Sgt. Pepper's Lonely Hearts Club Band?*

A. Richard Pryor
B. Bob Hope
C. George Burns

882 Which former Beatle was arrested for marijuana possession by Japanese authorities in 1980?

883 On what album does Paul McCartney's touching tribute to John Lennon, "Here Today," appear?

884 What duet with Paul McCartney on Michael Jackson's *Thriller* album helped secure that disc critical mainstream airplay—at a time when many non-R&B stations were still leery about playing Jackson's solo work?

885 Name the Paul McCartney duet with Michael Jackson that boasted a video in which both men appeared as traveling song-and-dance men.

886 What cameo role does George Harrison play in the film *Shanghai Surprise*?

887 For what consumer product was the song "Revolution" incorporated as part of a national ad campaign in 1987?

888 Which former Beatle, when asked in 1984 whether the members of his old band believed in reincarnation, replied "I'm sure John does!"?

889 On what LP did Paul McCartney team up with Elvis Costello?

890 Identify the Beatle who said this: "(Dealing with the press in the sixties) was worse because it was a new experience for me. But now I don't give a damn what you say about me, because I know who I am and I know what I feel. . . "

891 Which solo George Harrison LP, overseen by the same man who would produce the Beatles' reunion sessions, features a nostalgic look back at the group's history?

892 Who produced the first Traveling Wilburys album?

893 Paul McCartney composed a classical piece that was performed by the Liverpool Philharmonic Orchestra in the early '90s. Name it.

894 Name the 1993 film, set during the Beatles' early days in Hamburg, that features an eerily on-target performance from Ian Hart as the young (and furious) John Lennon.

895 Identify the speaker: "When I'm ninety-five, and it's *This Is Your Life* time, they'll still be referring to me as 'ex-Beatle.' None of us is ever going to lose that association. Sometimes we would like to, but then again it does have its advantages. It's still the best way I know to get a good table at a restaurant."

896 Identify the speaker: "It's not a great disaster. People keep talking about it as if it's the end of the earth. It's only a rock group that split up. It's nothing important."

897 Identify the speaker: "I remember thinking of it like army buddies. . . This idea that you've been army buddies, but one day you'll have to kiss the army good-bye and go on and get married, act like normal people. It was a bit like that for the Beatles."

898 Identify the speaker: "I like to be successful and popular, but there comes a point where it's unhealthy that people think you're something that you're not—and the next thing is that fans put you out on a trip, and limit what you may be in their eyes."

899 In what year will Paul McCartney turn sixty-four?

900 1995 marked the release of *The Beatles Anthology 1*, a collection featuring previously unreleased versions of Beatles songs that was a major commercial success. This was not the first such post-breakup release, however. Name the 1977 collection of previously unreleased versions of Beatles songs that was also a major commercial success.

901 For what project was the unfinished song "Free As A Bird" originally intended?

902 What snippet of Lennon-speak appears near the end of the Beatles' much-anticipated 1995 reunion song "Free As A Bird"? Identify the forwards *and* backwards messages.

903 What resolution of a long-delayed legal dispute supposedly inspired the composition of the song "Free As A Bird"?

904 True or false: The songwriting credit for the single "Free As A Bird" reads "Lennon/McCartney."

905 In 1996, when the Beatles' second reunion single "Real Love" was released, a vintage mid-sixties photograph was selected for the cover of the CD single release. What object was airbrushed out of this photograph, in deference to nineties sensibilities?

906 Name the former member of the Electric Light Orchestra who oversaw studio work on the reunion singles "Free As A Bird" and "Real Love."

907 What is the connection between the 1996 Beatles single "Real Love" and Elvis Presley's 1956 single "Heartbreak Hotel"?

908 As the closing credits concluded over the sound of studio outtakes, the 1995 televised documentary *The Beatles Anthology* issued its last words—via a remark from John Lennon that seemed strangely apropos of the "Free As A Bird" and "Real Love" singles. What did John say?

909 Identify the source of the following quote: "The world is still spinning and so are we and so are you. When the spinning stops, that'll be the time to worry, not before. Until then, the Beatles are alive and well and the beat goes on, the beat goes on."

Answers

794 George Harrison: "My Sweet Lord," 1970; Paul McCartney: "Uncle Albert/Admiral Halsey," 1970; Ringo Starr: "Photograph," 1973; John Lennon: "Whatever Gets You Through the Night," 1974.

795 Phil Spector

796 Paul McCartney: *McCartney,* 1970; George Harrison: *All Things Must Pass,* 1970; John Lennon: *Imagine,* 1970; Ringo Starr: *Ringo,* 1973.

797 "My Sweet Lord"

798 "Happy Christmas (War Is Over)"

799 *John Lennon/Plastic Ono Band*

800 "God," from *John Lennon/Plastic Ono Band*

801 The term referred to the loyal Beatles fans who dutifully loitered outside the Apple studios, seemingly in lieu of a professional career.

802 "I'd Have You Anytime"

803 Paul McCartney. The spat occurred during the often-acrimonious sessions for the album that would eventually see the light of day as *Let It Be.*

804 George Harrison and Phil Spector

805 "Another Day"

806 His 1968 conviction for possession of cannabis; there's little doubt, however, that his opposition to the Vietnam War earned him enemies at high levels within the American government.

807 Ravi Shankar

808 Bob Dylan came out of seclusion for his first major concert appearance in years.

809 Ringo Starr and George Harrison

810 Mick Jagger

811 "While My Guitar Gently Weeps," "Something," and "Here Comes The Sun."

812 "(We've Got To Relieve) Bangla Desh."

813 False. It only rose as high as #2.

814 Phil Spector, who received credit as coproducer of the album.

815 The venomous "How Do You Sleep?," perhaps the only song on that remarkable album that has not aged well.

816 A large pig

817 One beetle is, er, mating with another. Could this have been intended metaphorically?

818 The letters *L.I.L.Y.,* which presumably stand for "Linda I Love You."

819 "Dear Friend"

820 EMI Studios

821 Paul McCartney, via his band Wings

822 *Some Time In New York City*

823 *The New York Times*

824 True

825 False

826 None. McCartney opted instead to regale his audience with classics like "Bip Bop" and "Wild Life." John Lennon regularly featured "Come Together" in his stage act, and George Harrison included "Something" and "While My Guitar Gently Weeps" in his, but McCartney fans had to wait until 1975 to hear Paul's live renditions of such Beatles classics as "Lady Madonna," "Yesterday," and "Blackbird."

827 "Hi Hi Hi"

828 "Live And Let Die"

829 There were none. The anthem consists of three seconds of silence.

830 "C Moon"

831 a) "Young Americans"

832 *Band On The Run*

833 True. The song is "Picasso's Last Words Drink To Me," which appears on *Band On The Run*.

834 True. The bonus *Band On The Run* song in question is the superb "Helen Wheels."

835 True. Lennon, busily reestablishing his reputation as one of show business' least attractive drunks, had gotten more than a little unruly during a Smothers Brothers performance. Tom Smothers had joined in the joyous singalong of 1969's "Give Peace A Chance." His brother Dick was the primary target of Lennon's abuse.

836 *Rock 'n' Roll*

837 True. The song was "You Won't See Me."

838 False. Bowie did, however, tape a memorable version of "The Little Drummer Boy" with Crosby.

839 True

840 "#9 Dream," which first appeared on *Walls and Bridges*.

841 "Ah, bowakawa, poussé poussé."

842 *Mind Games*

843 *Rock 'n' Roll*

844 October 9. His son Sean shares the same birthday.

845 "All we are saying is give peace a chance."

846 "One After 909"

847 "Revolution 9"

848 The letter "o," which appears nine times in the names "John Ono Lennon" and "Yoko Ono Lennon."

849 "Whatever Gets You Through The Night," "Lucy In The Sky With Diamonds," and "I Saw Her Standing There."

850 Lennon had bet John that the single "Whatever Gets You Through The Night" would not reach the #1 spot in the United States. It did.

851 Yoko Ono. The couple, separated for a year and a half, reunited not long after the concert.

852 "Fame." The song's other writers were David Bowie and Carlos Alomar.

853 "Stand By Me"

854 Elephant's Memory

855 Alan Parsons, whose Alan Parsons Project met with international acclaim.

856 His son Sean was born.

857 1975

858 True. This occurred in early 1974; Lennon's legal worries would persist for some time longer.

859 True. The track in question is Elton John's mid-seventies cover of "Lucy In The Sky With Diamonds."

860 True. The single was "No No Song."

861 True. This took place in May of 1972, not, perhaps, Paul's best year. The single peaked at #28 in the United States.

862 True. It was the B side of the single that served as the follow-up to "No No Song."

863 False

864 True. It made it all the way to the #36 slot in the States, and is actually nowhere near as dumb as its title would lead you to believe.

865 *Ringo.* The songs in question: "Photograph" and "You're Sixteen."

866 All three; the four former Fabs never occupied the same studio at the same time, however. Of course, the same could be said for vast chunks of *The White Album*!

867 True; the film was *200 Motels* (1971).

868 False

869 True. The film was *Lisztomania* (1975).

870 True. The film was *Born To Boogie* (1972).

871 July 27, 1976

872 Lennon and Yoko Ono were honored guests at the inauguration of President Jimmy Carter.

873 The song was "Mull Of Kintyre," and it was available on the collection *Wings' Greatest*.

874 *Live! At The Star Club*

875 *Rock 'n' Roll Music*

876 "Got to Get You Into My Life." The followup "old single," "Ob-La-Di, Ob-La-Da," didn't fare as well for some reason.

877 Dirk McQuickly, perhaps the cutest Rutle

878 George Harrison

879 "Zzzzzzz"

880 *Beatlemania*. It wasn't the Beatles; it was an incredible simulation.

881 c) George Burns

882 Paul McCartney

883 *Tug Of War*

884 "The Girl Is Mine"

885 "Say Say Say"

886 He portrays a nightclub singer.

887 Nike athletic shoes

888 George Harrison

889 *Flowers In The Dirt*

890 George Harrison, during a tense 1986 joint press conference with Madonna.

891 *Cloud Nine.* The song was "When We Was Fab." The producer was Jeff Lynne.

892 Otis and Nelson Wilbury—codenames for Jeff Lynne and George Harrison.

893 *Liverpool Oratorio*

894 *Backbeat*

895 Ringo Starr

896 John Lennon. His tape-recorded remark appears near the end of the televised documentary *The Beatles Anthology.*

897 Paul McCartney, during an interview featured in the televised documentary *The Beatles Anthology.*

898 George Harrison

899 Paul McCartney will turn 64 on June 18, 2006.

900 *The Beatles At The Hollywood Bowl*

901 A film about the Lennons to be called *The Ballad Of John And Yoko.*

902 Forwards: "Made for John Lennon."
Backwards: "Turned out nice again. . . didn't
it?"

903 John Lennon's victory against those elements
of the United States government that sought
to deny him the right to live in the U.S.

904 False. It reads "Original composition by John
Lennon, Beatles version by John Lennon, Paul
McCartney, George Harrison, and Ringo
Starr."

905 Ringo's cigarette

906 Jeff Lynne, late of the Electric Light Orchestra
and the Traveling Wilburys.

907 On "Real Love," Paul McCartney played the
same stand-up double bass used for the
"Heartbreak Hotel" sessions.

908 "I'm ready to sing for the world, George, if
you'll just give me the backing." He seems to
have been speaking to producer George
Martin.

909 It is part of the final pre-breakup Beatles press
release.

BIBLIOGRAPHY

Brown, Peter, and Gaines, Steven. *The Love You Make: An Insider's Story of the Beatles.* Macmillan, 1983.

Carr, Roy, and Tyler, Tony. *The Beatles: An Illustrated Record,* Harmony Books, 1978.

Coleman, Ray. *Lennon.* McGraw-Hill, 1984.

Giuliano, Geoffrey. *The Lost Beatles Interviews.* Penguin, 1994.

Hertsgaard, Mark. *A Day in the Life: The Music and Artistry of the Beatles.* Dell, 1995.

Lewisohn, Mark. *The Beatles: Recording Sessions.* Harmony Books, 1988.

MacDonald, Ian. *Revolution in the Head.* Henry Holt, 1994.

Schaffner, Nicholas. *The Beatles Forever.* McGraw-Hill, 1978.

Solt, Andrew, and Egan, Sam. *Imagine: John Lennon.* Macmillan, 1988.

Wenner, Jann. *Lennon Remembers: The Rolling Stone Interviews.* Penguin, 1973.

BRANDON TOROPOV is a Boston–based writer whose other works include the play *An Undivided Heart* and the book *The I Ching for Beginners*. He has been listening to the Beatles, with varying degrees of obsession, since 1964.